Salesforce Field Service

A Beginner's Guide to Creating, Managing, and Automating Field Service

Saiteja Chatrati

Apress®

Salesforce Field Service: A Beginner's Guide to Creating, Managing, and Automating Field Service

Saiteja Chatrati
San Jose, CA, USA

ISBN-13 (pbk): 978-1-4842-9516-8   ISBN-13 (electronic): 978-1-4842-9517-5
https://doi.org/10.1007/978-1-4842-9517-5

Managing Director, Apress Media LLC: Welmoed Spahr
Acquisitions Editor: Susan McDermott
Development Editor: Laura Berendson
Coordinating Editor: Jessica Vakili

Distributed to the book trade worldwide by Springer Science+Business Media New York, 233 Spring Street, 6th Floor, New York, NY 10013. Phone 1-800-SPRINGER, fax (201) 348-4505, e-mail orders-ny@springer-sbm.com, or visit www.springeronline.com. Apress Media, LLC is a California LLC and the sole member (owner) is Springer Science + Business Media Finance Inc (SSBM Finance Inc). SSBM Finance Inc is a **Delaware** corporation.

For information on translations, please e-mail booktranslations@springernature.com; for reprint, paperback, or audio rights, please e-mail bookpermissions@springernature.com.

Apress titles may be purchased in bulk for academic, corporate, or promotional use. eBook versions and licenses are also available for most titles. For more information, reference our Print and eBook Bulk Sales web page at www.apress.com/bulk-sales.

Any source code or other supplementary material referenced by the author in this book is available to readers on the GitHub repository: https://github.com/Apress/Salesforce-Field-Service. For more detailed information, please visit https://www.apress.com/gp/services/source-code.

Paper in this product is recyclable

To my family for their unconditional love and support

Table of Contents

About the Author

Saiteja Chatrati has spent several years within the Salesforce ecosystem. Being in the consulting space, she got the opportunity to design complex end to end implementations for fortune 500 organizations as well as startups. Her expertise includes architecting, solution designing, product management, business analysis and quality assurance.

You can learn more about her by visiting her LinkedIn page at https://www.linkedin.com/in/chatrati/.

About the Technical Reviewers

Heather Negley is an independent Salesforce consultant and author of the *Salesforce Consultant's Guide*. She is currently working with Simplus. She also mentors and coaches Salesforce professionals on consulting best practices. She is a results-driven, senior leader with more than 25 years of software, automation, and web experience in the private sector, nonprofits, and government. She is Salesforce and PMP certified and has worked on dozens of Salesforce implementations as a technology lead, project manager, business analyst, change manager, and solution and business architect.

Harshala Shewale is a UK-based certified Salesforce architect working with Accenture, specializing in the field service industry. She has more than 13 years of experience in solution design, consulting, and business transformation. She has worked across several industries such as manufacturing, energy and utilities, healthcare, etc., and has led several Salesforce implementations worldwide.

CHAPTER 1

Introducing Salesforce Field Service

In its most basic form, a *field service* is any service provided outside the organization's boundaries. In field service, resources are dispatched at the site to perform one-time or recurring tasks such as delivery, inspections, repairs, installation, maintenance, etc. The use cases of a field service could span anything from fixing a laundry machine at home to performing annual maintenance service of your car to repairing medical equipment at a hospital.

In this chapter, you will learn about the entire field service life cycle and understand how Salesforce can help in managing the entire process. We will cover the following topics:

- Field service players and life cycle

- Field service challenges

- Why use Salesforce Field Service?

- Salesforce Field Service use cases

- Components of Salesforce Field Service

© Saiteja Chatrati 2023
S. Chatrati, *Salesforce Field Service*, https://doi.org/10.1007/978-1-4842-9517-5_1

- The relationship between Salesforce Service Cloud and Salesforce Field Service

- Enabling Salesforce Field Service

By the end of this chapter, you should be able to understand the basics of Salesforce Field Service and understand how it can be leveraged to automate the entire field service process.

In today's competitive world, a smooth, fast, and efficient service process is extremely crucial for any business for customer retention and loyalty. Organizations with field service often involve direct customer interaction. Since customers now have more options than ever, recurring delays and unpleasant experiences with service can lead customers to look for another option. The majority of the decision-makers believe that service resources are the face of their brand, so companies need streamlined field service management solutions that can boost a service resource's productivity by providing optimized scheduling and mobile capabilities from anywhere that provide seamless connections with the customers. Without an intelligent field service management system, organizations would not be able to keep up with the modern standards.

Let's start by understanding different players involved in the Salesforce Field Service world.

Field Service Players

Five players are actively involved in the entire life cycle of Salesforce Field Service: administrator, service agent, dispatcher, technician, and manager. Let's dive deep into the responsibilities for each role (see Table 1-1).

Table 1-1. *Field Service Players*

Player	Responsibilities
Administrator	Administrators are responsible for managing and maintaining the Salesforce Field Service platform. They configure the platform, manage user access, and ensure data accuracy and security.
Service agent	Service agents are responsible for interacting with customers and addressing any incoming customer cases. Service agents can create or request work orders according to the case details. They also book service appointments from the service console.
Dispatcher	Dispatchers are responsible for planning, scheduling, and dispatching service appointments to a service resource or group of service resources using the dispatcher console.
Service resource	Service resources are responsible for completing the tasks or jobs assigned to them. They use the Field Service mobile app to update job details and maintain accurate records. Service resources can work independently or in a group called *crew*.
Service manager	Service managers oversee the overall field service operations. They use the Salesforce Field Service platform to track performance metrics, manage budgets, and identify areas for improvement.

Important Note   Players and their responsibilities can sometimes overlap depending on the structure and size of the organization. For example, an organization that does not have a dispatcher could have the service agent perform the responsibilities of the dispatcher.

Field Service Life Cycle

The *Field Service life cycle* refers to a set of stages that a service request goes through (see Figure 1-1). The life cycle typically includes the following stages from creation to completion:

- *Service request or case creation*: The first stage is the creation of the service request or case. This can be initiated by a customer, a service agent, or a connected device.

- *Work order creation*: Work orders can be created manually or automatically, depending on the source of the request. Work orders include important information such as the customer name, location, and type of work.

- *Scheduling*: Once a work order is created, it needs to be scheduled. A service appointment is generated manually or automatically and holds all the information about the schedule of work order such as start time, end time, location, etc. Scheduling can be done manually or automatically using Salesforce's scheduling tools.

- *Dispatching*: The dispatching stage involves assigning the service appointment to a service resource and providing them with all the necessary information to complete the job.

- *Service delivery*: The service resource arrives on-site and performs the necessary work. During this stage, the service resource may need to communicate with the customer or other team members to resolve any issues that arise.

- *Job completion and tracking*: Once the work is complete, the service resource updates the job status in the Salesforce Field Service mobile app, records any parts used, and generates any necessary invoices or reports. This allows managers to track job progress and ensure that work is completed on time and within budget. Once the work order is completed, the related case is closed by the service resource, dispatcher, or agent.

- *Follow-up and feedback*: After the job is complete, follow-up and feedback are necessary to ensure customer satisfaction. This can include gathering feedback from the customer about the quality of service provided and making any necessary improvements to the field service process to ensure continued customer satisfaction.

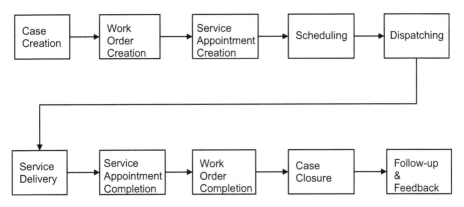

Figure 1-1. *Field service life cycle*

The field service life cycle is a critical process that must be managed effectively to ensure timely and high-quality service delivery. The Salesforce Field Service platform provides a wide range of tools and features to help organizations automate and optimize the field service life cycle, resulting in improved efficiency, productivity, and customer satisfaction.

Field Service Challenges

Multiple challenges might affect efficiency and customer satisfaction in field service operations. The following are some of the common field service challenges:

- *Time-consuming and error-prone*: Manual processes are often time-consuming and can lead to errors, particularly when dealing with large amounts of data or complex workflows. This can result in delays, rework, and lost productivity.

- *Inefficient scheduling*: Scheduling field service appointments manually can be challenging and often results in inefficient routing, which leads to wasted time and resources.

- *Lack of visibility*: Manual processes can make it difficult to track the status of service appointments in real time, leading to delays in communication and reduced visibility into the field service process.

- *Poor communication*: Communication between field technicians and dispatchers can be challenging when relying on manual processes, which can lead to misunderstandings and delays in resolving issues.

- *Limited data insights*: Manual processes often provide limited data insights into field service operations, making it difficult to identify trends, optimize processes, and make data-driven decisions.

- *Customer satisfaction*: Meeting customer expectations is one of the biggest challenges faced by field service providers. Manual processes can result in inconsistent service quality, particularly when dealing with complex or high-risk jobs, which can negatively impact customer satisfaction.

- *No transparency*: Without an efficient service tracking and notification system, customers have no visibility into when and by whom the work order will be completed.

- *Reduced scalability*: Manual processes are often limited in their ability to scale as a business grows, leading to challenges in managing and coordinating field service operations.

- *Technical knowledge*: Field service workers need to have a deep understanding of the products or services they are working with to be able to identify and resolve issues accurately. Lack of technical knowledge can lead to inefficiencies, delays, and errors.

- *Travel management*: Field service team members often have to travel to different job sites throughout the day. It can be challenging to manage travel routes effectively.

- *Safety*: Field service workers often work in hazardous environments, such as construction sites, power plants, or industrial facilities. They need to follow strict safety protocols to avoid accidents and injuries.

- *Remote support*: When field service workers encounter complex problems that they cannot solve on-site, they may need remote support from their colleagues or managers. Poor connectivity or technical issues can hinder effective remote support, leading to further delays and frustrations.

- *Data management*: Field service workers generate a lot of data, such as work orders, reports, and customer feedback. Managing large chunks of data can be challenging.

- *Workload balancing*: Field service workers need to balance their workload to ensure that they are meeting customer demands and deadlines while avoiding burnout. This requires effective planning and prioritization skills.

- *Inventory management*: Having limited visibility into inventory levels and movement can result in stockouts, overstocking, and inefficient use of inventory. This requires an organized inventory management system that can be updated from time to time to maintain accurate inventory levels.

To overcome these challenges, many organizations are turning to digital field service management solutions that provide automated workflows, real-time visibility, and data insights to optimize and streamline field service operations. In the next topic, let's understand the capabilities offered by Salesforce Field Service that can help in coping up with these challenges and improving the overall field service performance.

Why Salesforce Field Service?

Salesforce Field Service offers a range of capabilities to help companies manage their field service operations effectively. These are some of the key capabilities of Salesforce Field Service:

- *Scheduling automation and optimization*: To overcome scheduling challenges, Salesforce Field Service provides automation and optimization that recommends qualified service resources for scheduling based on their skills, availability, and location. The platform's AI-powered scheduling engine can also take into account factors such as traffic, weather, and technician preferences to optimize the schedule.

- *Dispatcher console*: Salesforce Field Service provides an efficient way to manage scheduling and dispatching via an intelligent workspace called the dispatcher console. The dispatcher console in Salesforce Field Service provides a centralized location for dispatchers to manage work orders and schedules, communicate with technicians, and make real-time decisions to ensure efficient field service operations.

- *Mobile anytime*: Service resources can access essential information on the go even when they are offline. All the safety protocols, specific instruction guidelines knowledge articles, and inventory required can be accessed through mobile devices from anywhere. Customer e-signatures can be digitally captured from a mobile device without relying on old-school paper processes.

- *Provide service from anywhere using a visual remote assistant*: To reduce in-person visits, mobile users can provide remote assistance using an integrated visual remote assistant. This feature allows mobile workers to connect in real time with their customers through a virtual guided interaction. Customers can be reached through a smart device from anywhere.

- *Appointment assistance*: Using appointment assistance, customers can track the real-time location of the mobile workers and receive messages about the estimated arrival time, increasing customer trust and reducing no-shows. Appointment assistance allows customers to create, update, cancel, or reschedule appointments through a self-service portal.

- *Efficient inventory management*: With Salesforce Field Service inventory management, businesses can gain real-time visibility into inventory levels, stock movements, and replenishment status. This allows businesses to make informed decisions and respond quickly to inventory issues.

- *Einstein AI to improve the first-time fix rate*: Einstein image recognition helps in recognizing assets or parts in images and suggests relevant articles or instructions instantly to service resources, which can help them in fixing issues at a faster rate.

- *Field service analytics*: Using field service analytics, service managers can visualize all the data in one platform, which helps in making better data-driven decisions. The Field Service Analytics app creates prebuilt dashboards based on your field service data that helps managers get more insights into the field service performance and key performance indicators (KPIs).

Salesforce Field Service Use Cases

Salesforce Field Service is a versatile platform that can be customized to meet the needs of various industries that have field service operations such as automotive, transportation, manufacturing, retail, consumer goods, waste management, insurance, healthcare, life sciences, financial services, real estate, telecommunication, information technology, food delivery, and much more. The following are some use cases of how Salesforce Field Service can benefit different industries.

Use Case: Automotive

Salesforce Field Service can help automobile industries increase efficiency by automating routine tasks, such as appointment scheduling, inventory management, and dispatching technicians. This reduces the need for manual intervention and saves time. Automobile companies can increase productivity by optimizing technician routes, reducing travel time, and minimizing the need for unnecessary visits. This results in greater operational efficiency and cost savings. Salesforce Field Service provides real-time tracking of inventory levels, enabling automobile dealers to monitor their inventory in real time. This helps to avoid running out of stock and ensures that technicians have the parts they need to complete their jobs. Preventive maintenance tasks, such as oil changes and tire rotations, can be scheduled automatically at regular intervals, based on the manufacturer's recommendations or customer requirements. This helps to ensure that vehicles are serviced on time, reducing the risk of breakdowns and extending the life of the vehicle.

Use Case: Real Estate

Virtual property tours can be handled using real-time video calling in the Salesforce Field Service mobile app. The real estate industry can use Salesforce Field Service to manage the maintenance of properties, including scheduling and tracking tasks such as repairs, cleaning, and landscaping. Salesforce Field Service can be used to manage their field workforce, including scheduling, dispatching, and tracking their activities. An inventory of maintenance supplies, tools, and equipment can be managed efficiently to ensure that field workforce has what they need to perform their tasks. Property management firms can use Salesforce Field Service to track the maintenance history of their properties and assets, ensuring that they are kept in good condition. Salesforce Field Service can be used to provide real-time updates to customers about the status of their property maintenance requests and to provide them with information about their properties and assets.

Use Case: Healthcare and Life Sciences

Salesforce Field Service can help healthcare organizations improve patient care by enabling them to respond quickly to patient needs. With Salesforce Field Service, healthcare organizations can schedule appointments, dispatch technicians, and provide real-time updates to patients about their appointments. Hospitals can enhance compliance by ensuring that healthcare professionals have the right certifications and training to perform their duties. This helps to improve quality and reduce the risk of noncompliance. In dire situations, healthcare professionals can have all the important information such as patient history, emergency contacts, nearby ambulance providers, or safety protocols handy even when offline using the Field Service mobile app. Ambulance providers can enable geolocation tracking so patients can track the live status of the ambulance route.

Use Case: Food and Beverages

Restaurants and food delivery businesses can use Salesforce Field Service to manage their delivery operations. They can use the platform to track deliveries in real time, manage driver schedules, and optimize routes to ensure timely delivery of orders. With Salesforce Field Service, businesses can use data analytics to optimize delivery routes, reducing travel time and fuel costs. The platform can also provide drivers with turn-by-turn directions to help them navigate to each delivery location efficiently.

Salesforce Field Service offers real-time tracking of delivery drivers, allowing businesses to monitor delivery progress and respond quickly to any issues that may arise. Salesforce Field Service can help businesses manage delivery exceptions such as missed deliveries, damaged goods, or customer complaints. The platform allows businesses to quickly respond to these issues and resolve them before they impact customer satisfaction.

These are only a handful of the numerous use cases available for Salesforce Field Service. The platform can be tailored according to the specific needs of organizations that depend on efficient field service management.

Components of Salesforce Field Service

The platform is composed of three key components that work together to provide end-to-end visibility and control over field service operations.

- Core Field Service features

- Field Service managed package

- Field Service mobile app

Enable the core Field Service features first; then install the managed package and mobile app as necessary.

- Core Field Service

  Once you enable Salesforce Field Service, the core objects and features are accessible to start configuring as per the business needs. Table 1-2 describe these core features.

Table 1-2. *Salesforce Field Service Core Features*

	Feature	Description
Related to work	Work orders	Field service job requests
	Work types	Templates for common field service work
	Service appointments	Appointments for field service work
	Maintenance plans	Used for tracking preventive maintenance
	Service report templates	Templates for customer reports
Related to service resources	Service resources	Mobile employees who can perform field service work
	Service crews	Group of service resources
	Service territories	Regions where field service work is performed
	Skills	Skills required to perform field service tasks
Related to time	Operating hours	Times when field service work can be performed
	Shifts	Shifts are used to extend operating hours
	Time sheets	To track the time field service employees are spending on tasks or travel
Related to Inventory	Products items	Parts stored in inventory location
	Products requests	To track requests for parts
	Product transfers	To track transfers of parts between locations.
	Return orders	To track returning parts

You will learn about these objects in Chapter 2.

- Field Service managed package

  Install the managed package after enabling
  Salesforce Field Service to get access to the
  dispatcher console, scheduling tools, a variety of
  custom objects, and guided setup. Installing the
  managed package is covered in Chapter 3.

- Field Service mobile app

  The mobile app comes with offline capability,
  which means mobile users can continue working
  even when there is no Internet connectivity.
  The Field Service mobile app can be tailored to
  build varied features that Salesforce Field Service
  provides such as push notifications, geolocation
  tracking, appointment assistance, knowledge
  integration, inventory management, service reports
  management, and much more. This app is available
  on the Apple Store and Google Play. Learn to
  configure the Field Service mobile app in Chapter 7.

Table 1-3 summarizes varied capabilities of each component for
admins, agents, dispatchers, and mobile workers.

Table 1-3. *Salesforce Field Service Components*

Core Field Service	Field Service Managed Package	Field Service Mobile App
Once Field Service is enabled from setup, admins and agents can do the following:	Once the Field Service managed package is installed, dispatchers can do the following:	Once the Field Service Mobile App is setup, mobile workers can do the following:
• Configure core Field Service objects. Set up service appointments, work orders, operating hours, locations, and skills as per the business needs. • Enabling Field Service will turn on geocoding, which helps in tracking the real-time location of mobile workers. • Manage the inventory required to perform field service. • Enable the Salesforce mobile app to provide workers with mobile access. • Analyze field service data through reports and dashboards.	• Get a 360-degree view of all service appointments, open slots, available service resources, real-time maps, and much more all within the dispatcher console. • Optimize scheduling policies according to the business needs. • Get service resource recommendations based on skills, location, scheduling policies, work types, etc.	• View appointments, location maps, work orders, and customer details. • Complete service reports from a mobile device and get an e-signature from the customer once the work order is complete. • Track any inventory required to complete the task. • View any knowledge articles, instruction manuals, and suggestions relevant to the task. • Receive push notifications.

Relationship Between Salesforce Service Cloud and Field Service

Salesforce Service Cloud and Field Service are both designed to help businesses manage their customer service operations, but they serve different purposes.

Salesforce Service Cloud enables businesses to manage customer interactions across multiple channels, including email, phone, chat, and social media. It includes features such as case management, knowledge management, and customer self-service, and it is designed to help businesses within office boundaries.

Salesforce Field Service is an extension of Service Cloud. In Field Service, services are offered in the field beyond office boundaries. Usually, businesses use both Service Cloud and Field Service if they offer both in-house and on-site customer service.

Field Service is associated with Service Cloud through the Case object. Field Service's Work Order object is related to Case through a lookup relationship. Lookup relationships allow one object to be associated to another object in a one-to-many fashion. This relationship is loosely coupled. Figure 1-2 demonstrates the relationship between the Case and Work Order objects.

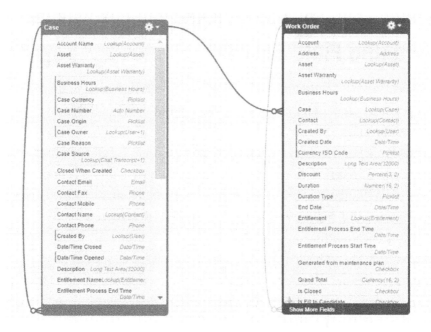

Figure 1-2. *Relationship between Case and Work Order*

As shown in Figure 1-2, a Case can have many Work Orders. Since it is loosely coupled, even if the Case is deleted, the associated Work Order is not deleted or vice versa.

Because Field Service is built on top of Service Cloud, several capabilities overlap. Table 1-4 describes some of the capabilities that are similar to both Service Cloud and Field Service.

Table 1-4. *Service Cloud and Field Service Comparison*

Feature	Service Cloud	Field Service
Knowledge	Knowledge articles can be attached to a case to provide additional guidelines and specifications for service agents.	Knowledge articles can be attached to work orders, work order line items, and work types to provide additional guidelines and specifications for field technicians.
Entitlement management	Entitlements are used to track SLA's for the cases.	Entitlements are used to track SLA for the work orders.
Milestones	Milestones are set up on case to track required steps in a service process, for example, first response time.	Milestones are set up on work order to track required steps in a field service process, for example, average repair time.
Asset Management	Assets are set up on a case to track purchased or installed products by customer.	Assets are set up on work orders to track purchased or installed products by customer.

Enabling Salesforce Field Service

Knowing the importance of implementing Salesforce Field Service, it's time to enable Field Service for your organization. It's always advisable to first implement and exhaustively test configurations in a sandbox or testing environment before deploying them to the production environment. Use the Developer Edition account to practice with Field Service. The developer environment is a free, full-featured copy of the platform. If you have not already created a Developer Edition account, navigate to this link `https://developer.salesforce.com/signup` and sign up. Once you sign up, you will receive an email to verify your account and set up a password. If you already created developer environment, log in with your username and password using `https://login.salesforce.com/`.

Once you have successfully logged into the developer environment, follow these steps to enable Field Service:

1. Navigate to Setup and search for *Field Service* in the Quick Find box. Click Field Service Settings (see Figure 1-3).

2. Click the toggle button to enable Field Service.

Figure 1-3. *Enabling Field Service*

Hurray! You just enabled Salesforce Field Service. You now have access to all the core objects and fields within Field Service. Using these core objects, you can manage work orders, design service territories, and handle a workforce.

Summary

Overall, Salesforce Field Service is a customer service product built on top of Service Cloud that helps businesses in scheduling, dispatching, and optimizing field service operations.

- The Salesforce Field Service platform provides a collaborative environment that enables communication among the different players involved. The players include the administrator, service agent, dispatcher, technician, and manager.

- The Field Service life cycle typically involves a service agent or customer who will open a case for a service request. If the request requires field service operation, a work order is created. A service appointment holding the schedule information is created, scheduled, and dispatched to an available field service resource who can arrive at the site, complete the job, and close the work order.

- As organizations grow, their field service operations and team members face challenges in different aspects including scheduling, visibility, data, travel, inventory, safety, scalability, etc. Salesforce offers a wide range of capabilities that can help overcome these challenges.

- Some of the capabilities of Salesforce include automatic scheduling and optimization, offline mobile support, visual remote assistant, appointment assistant, efficient inventory management, Einstein analytics, and AI powering.

- Salesforce Field Service can be used for multiple industries including automotive, real estate, food, and delivery businesses.

- Salesforce Field Service comprises three main components: the core Field Service, the managed package, and the Field Service mobile app.

In the next chapter, you will learn the core objects and relationships in Salesforce Field Service through a data model.

CHAPTER 2

Salesforce Field Service Objects and Data Model

In the previous chapter, you learned why Salesforce Field Service is important to your business and how to enable it. In this chapter, we will cover the objects and data model in Salesforce Field Service. Salesforce Field Service involves multiple objects that are interdependent with each other. Once you enable Field Service, you should be able to access these core objects. With the help of a data model, you will understand how these objects are interlinked with each other.

To execute crucial field service operations such as handling work orders, service regions, and monitoring your staff, Field Service's core objects are used.

While there are numerous objects within the Field Service umbrella, the good news is that they can all be categorized into six buckets, called the six Ws (see Figure 2-1).

- **What** work is to be performed
- **Who** performs the work
- **Where** the work is performed

© Saiteja Chatrati 2023
S. Chatrati, *Salesforce Field Service*, https://doi.org/10.1007/978-1-4842-9517-5_2

- **When** the work is performed

- **With what**

- **For whom**

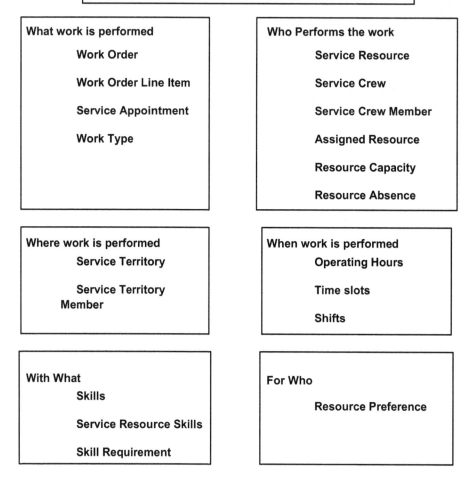

Figure 2-1. *Salesforce Field Service core objects*

Figure 2-2 represents the interrelationships between the core objects.

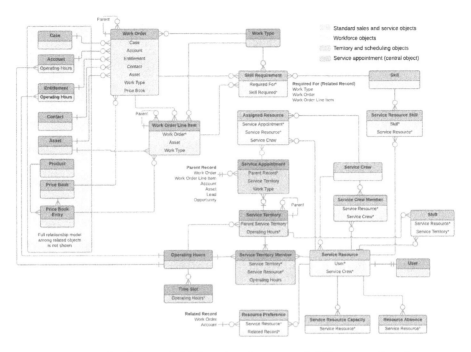

Figure 2-2. *Salesforce Field Service data model(Source: developer. salesforce.com)*

Let's take a closer look at each of these categories and the objects.

What Work Is to Be Performed

This category includes all the objects that are used to define the job structure, time schedule, templates, and skills required to perform the task.

Work orders are important for any field service business. A **work order** suggests work to be completed for your customers. For example, a customer would submit a work order to perform a multipoint inspection for their car.

A work order can be further divided into subtasks to be performed in sequence. These subtasks are called **work order line items**. For example, if the work order is a multipoint car inspection, then the work order line items could be as follows:

- Work order line item 1 for fluid levels check

- Work order line item 2 for tires check

- Work order line item 3 for brakes check and so on

The work order and work order line items share a *master-detail* relationship. This means, a work order and a work order line item are tightly coupled. Deleting the parent work order would delete the related work order line items as well.

A work order can be added to multiple sales and service object records including the following:

- Assets, to keep track of the work done on a certain asset.

- Accounts and contacts, to keep track of customers.

- Cases, to keep track of work performed for customer cases.

- Entitlements and service contracts, to keep track of work performed as part of the service-level agreement.

- Price books, to link items in the price books with work orders and their line items if you've built up a product catalog in Salesforce to manage the goods and services you provide. Each work order line item on a work order can be linked to a price book entry (product) in a price book if the work order includes a price book.

If the work order represents what work is to be performed, the **service appointment** indicates the scheduling details such as appointment duration, arrival window, and scheduled start and end times of the work to be performed. Each service appointment has a parent work order or work order line item. Work order or work order line items can have child service appointments to track multiple visits. You can also add child service appointments to Account, Asset, Lead, and Opportunity if you need to track relevant visit information. Service appointment information is used to optimize the schedule. Schedule optimization is covered in detail in Chapter 4.

If your team performs the same job repeatedly, you can create a **work type** to standardize the process. Work types are templates that can be applied to work orders or work order line items. Work types can be used to define the duration of the work. You can also define the skills and products required to complete the work in the work type.

Who Performs the Work

This category bundles up all the objects that are related to users or resources that would be performing the field work.

Your workforce is referred to as **service resources** in Salesforce. Service resources are assigned to service appointments to complete a field service job.

In some cases, a team of service resources is required to complete a task. In such situations, **service crews** can be used to create a group of service resources with supporting skills and assign them to appointments as a unit.

Service resources that are part of a service crew are called **service crew members**. Service crew members can be added to the service crew using the service crew list or crew management tool.

An **assigned resource** represents a service resource who is assigned to a service appointment. Assigned resources appear in the assigned resources related list on the service appointments object.

The hourly or job-based capacity of contractors is tracked in the **resource capacity** records. Resource capacity indicates the maximum number of scheduled appointments or maximum number of scheduled hours that a capacity based service resource can complete within a specific time period.

The **resource absence** is used to track the time when a resource is unavailable. Service resources aren't assigned to appointments during schedule optimization that conflict with their absences.

Where the Work Is Performed

This bucket of objects is related to the geographical region where the work is performed.

The geographic areas in which your staff can execute field service work are known as **service territories**. A service territory can have child territory to represent regional hierarchy.

Service territory members are resources who work within the territory. Associating service territory members to a service territory ensures that resources are assigned appointments near their home base. A resource can be assigned to one or more territories.

On some occasions, service resources need to be available to take on work in more than one service territory. Service resources can have only one primary territory but multiple secondary territories.

When the Work Is Performed

This category includes all the objects that represent the time when the team is available to perform the task.

Operating hours represent when your team performs work. Operating hours can be set up for accounts, service territories, service territory members, and appointment booking.

Time slots include details of the operating hours. They represent a window of time on a specific day of the week when work can be done. One or more time slots make up the operating hours.

Service resources can plan and modify their constantly shifting work schedules through **shifts**. Shifts are similar to operating hours with some differences. Operating hours let you define consistent time slots, whereas shifts let you define varying time slots that can vary from day to day. Operation hours and shifts both can be used together to assign work to team members as needed. For instance, you can define shifts to specify weekend on-call tasks and use operating hours for your usual weekday hours.

With What

This bucket defines all the objects related to skills that are required by the resources to complete a specific work order.

Skills represent qualifications, certifications, or areas of expertise of your workforce.

The skills held by a service resource are represented by a **service resource skill**. All service resources in your organization can have skills assigned to them so that you can see their certifications and areas of specialization as well as their skill levels, which range from 0 to 99.99. You may, for instance, attribute John with level 70 for the Installation skill or level 40 for expertise in the Spanish skill.

Skills needed to execute a task are known as **skill requirements**. Skill requirements can be added to work type, work order, and work order line item as a related list.

For Whom

This category represents customers for whom work is performed. Customer information is held in account and contact records in Salesforce. Sometimes customers have preferences for the service resource they want. **Resource preference** is used to represent a specific service resource as required, preferred, or excluded. This is to ensure good customer service by matching the best resource to the job. The resource preference can be added to accounts, work orders, work order line item, location, and assets.

These are some of the key objects and relationships in the Salesforce Field Service data model. Organizations can further expand the data model by developing custom objects to incorporate more business-specific needs.

Summary

Even though numerous objects fall under the Salesforce Field Service umbrella, the core objects can be categorized into six groups.

- What work is performed is tracked using work orders, work order line items, service appointments, and work type object records. These objects collectively hold the nature and schedule of the work.

- Who performs the work is tracked using service resources, service crew, service crew members, assigned resources, resource capacity, and resource absence. These objects are used to keep record of all the information related to the resources who will be contributing to the field service work.

- Service territories represent the geographical locations where the work is performed, and service territory members represent resources who work within the region.

- The timeframe when the team is available to perform the task is tracked using operating hours, time slots, and shifts.

- The skills held by a service resource are represented by a service resource object. Skills represent your workforce's expertise. Some tasks may need special skills; these skills are tracked using the skill requirement object.

- Account and contact object records hold the information of the customer requesting the service. Sometimes customers may request professionals of their choice. This can be handled by adding the preferred resources to the customer account. Preferred resources can also be added to assets, locations, work orders, and work order line items.

Now that you know the basics of Salesforce Field Service, in the next chapter, you will learn how to implement Field Service step-by-step according to your organization needs.

CHAPTER 3

Step-by-Step Field Service Implementation

Buckle up! Now that you know the incredible advantages of using Salesforce Field Service, it's time to get your hands dirty with the actual implementation. Previously, you learned the core Field Service objects can be categorized into the following six Ws: **who does, what, where, when, for whom, and with what.** You will learn how to configure these Ws in this chapter.

This chapter will walk you through setting up Salesforce Field Service step-by-step with an example business use case. The following topics will be covered:

- Enabling Salesforce Field Service

- Installing the managed package

- Managing Field Service permission set licenses

- Assigning page layouts

- Checking data integration rules

- Using the guided setup

- Setting up service territories and operating hours

© Saiteja Chatrati 2023

S. Chatrati, *Salesforce Field Service*, https://doi.org/10.1007/978-1-4842-9517-5_3

- Setting up work types and skills

- Setting up service resources

- Setting up dispatchers and agents

- Customizing appointment bookings

- Customizing scheduling policies

- Creating work orders

By the end of this chapter, you should be able to configure Salesforce Field Service for your business.

Field Service Business Use Case

ABC Automobiles is an automotive dealer and service provider. They offer services for all of their asset groups including SUVs, sedans, electric vehicles, crossovers, and trucks. With service centers located across the United States, they offer a wide range of service options ranging from a simple oil change to full-circle multipoint inspections.

The following are some of the examples of types of services the service center offers:

- Recall

- Oil and filter change

- Tire rotation

- Battery performance test

- Repair or replace parts

- Four-wheel alignment

- Air conditioning service

- Brake fluid test

Each type of service has specific skill requirements and is performed by certified and skilled technicians.

Their power workforce consists of the following:

- *Salesforce admin*: Responsible for setting up Field Service for ABC automobiles.

- *Service agent*: Responsible for logging customer inquiries and appointments.

- *Dispatcher*: Responsible for managing and assigning the service appointments to the right technicians. The dispatcher will be using the dispatcher console to manage the service appointments.

- *Mobile technicians*: Skilled technicians who will be acting on the work orders. Technicians will be using their mobile device to track and complete work orders.

Step into the shoes of an admin and follow along to set up Salesforce Field Service for ABC Automobiles.

Enable Field Service

To start using Field Service, we need to enable it.

To enable Field Service, follow these steps:

1. From Setup, in the Quick Find box, search for and select Field Service Settings.

2. Click the toggle button to enable Field Service (see Figure 3-1).

Figure 3-1. *Enabling Field Service*

3. Once you have enabled Field Service, update the settings shown in Figure 3-2 and click Save.

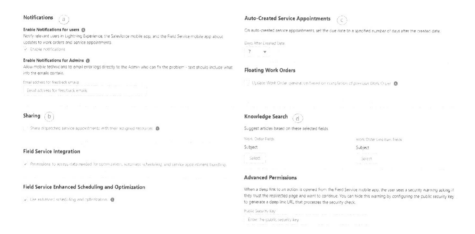

Figure 3-2. *Field Service settings*

a. Under Notifications, do the following:

–   Select the Enable Notifications checkbox if you want to turn on in-app notifications for Lightning Experience, Salesforce mobile devices, and Field Service mobile users.

–   Enter the admin's email address if you want to enable notifications for admins to receive error logs from the Field Service mobile app.

Note   In-app notifications are sent to users when the following actions occur on a work order or work order line item that they own or follow:

A text or file post is added.

A tracked field is updated.

The record owner changes.

The resource assignments change on a related service appointment.

Child records of work orders are created or deleted.

Notifications of child records of work orders are sent only if the option to track all related objects is selected in your feed tracking settings for work orders.

---

b. Under Sharing, optionally select the checkbox for sharing service appointments with assigned resources.

c. While setting up work type, you can opt to create new service appointments automatically for work orders and work order line items. Under Auto Created Service Appointments, configure the number of days between the created date and the due date on autocreated service appointments.

d. If you want to suggest knowledge articles, select the fields for work orders and work order line items. Selected fields will be scanned by the search engine to recommend relevant knowledge articles.

Install the Field Service Managed Package

Installing the managed package will open up all the following features for users to access:

- *Guided setup:* Guided setup is a handy tool that makes your life easier by walking you through configuring many Field Service tasks such as setting up service territories, setting up service resources, setting up work types, assigning permissions, configuring appointments booking, optimizing schedules, etc.

- *Scheduling optimization*: Optimize the schedule for your workforce by scheduling appointments based on your business objective, rules, skills, availability, and location.

- *Dispatcher console*: The dispatcher console provides a bird's-eye view of all the field service appointments and available service resources for dispatchers to easily schedule appointments. The dispatcher console provides a Gantt chart and an interactive map to monitor appointments in real time.

- *Field Service admin app*: This is a one-stop shop to manage optimization, customize the dispatcher console, and update managed package settings.

After Field Service is enabled, install the managed package. To install the managed package, follow these steps:

1. Click the installation link to install the managed package in a sandbox or production organization.

   ```
   https://fsl.secure.force.com/install
   ```

2. If asked, enter your login credentials.

3. Select Install for Admins Only.

4. Check the acknowledgment box for installing a non-Salesforce application.

5. If you are asked to approve third-party access, select Yes and then Continue. This will grant access to third-party websites for geolocation and optimization services (see Figure 3-3).

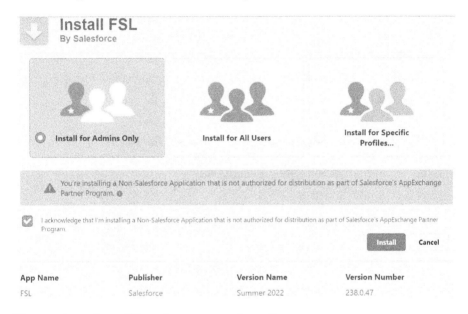

Figure 3-3. *Installing the managed package*

6. If you receive a warning that installation is taking longer, click Done and wait for the email.

    Once the package is installed, two new applications are added to the App Launcher.

    - *Field Service app*: This app is for dispatchers to manage the dispatcher console.

- *Field Service admin app*: This app is for admins. It includes the Field Service Settings tab to access guided setup and configure field service operations.

Manage Field Service Permissions Set Licenses

Creating and assigning permissions to users is a required step for users to access various features and functions of Field Service.

Field Service offers various licenses and permissions for specific needs. Table 3-1 lists the different licenses and permissions that are required for different personas.

Table 3-1. *Required Permissions for Different Personas*

Persona	Permission Sets and Licenses	Description
Admin	• Field Service Admin License* • FSL Admin permissions	Allows admins to manage all the Field Service objects, the Field Service admin app, Field Service Visualforce pages, and logic services.
Agent	• Field Service Agent License* • FSL Agent permissions	Allows agents to create, book, and schedule service appointments using the global actions.

(continued)

Table 3-1. (*continued*)

Persona	Permission Sets and Licenses	Description
Resource	• Field Service Mobile License • Field Service Scheduling License • FSL Resource permissions	A Field Service mobile license is required for using the Field Service mobile app. The Field Service Scheduling License is required for resources to be visible on the Gantt chart and be scheduled by the scheduling engine. FSL Resource Permissions is required for users to update appointment status and location.
Dispatcher	• Field Service Dispatcher License • FSL Dispatcher permissions	Allows dispatchers to use the dispatcher console for scheduling, optimizing, and dispatching service appointments. Dispatchers can view global actions and related objects.
Community Dispatcher	• Field Service Community Dispatcher License • FSL Community Dispatcher permissions	Allows community users to use the dispatcher console for scheduling, optimizing, and dispatching service appointments. Community dispatchers can view global actions and related objects.

(*continued*)

Table 3-1. (*continued*)

Persona	Permission Sets and Licenses	Description
Mobile Technicians	• Field Service Mobile License • Field Service Resource License • FSL Resource permissions	Allows resources to use the Field Service mobile app.
Customer	• Field Service Self Service License • FSL Self Service permissions	Customers view all global actions and their related objects to create, book, and schedule their appointments on the Experience Builder site.
Integration User	• Field Service Integration	Allows users to access data needed for optimization, automatic scheduling, and service appointment bundling.
Field Service Bundle for Dispatcher	• Field Service Bundle for Dispatcher License • FSL Bundle for Dispatcher permissions	Allows users to bundle service appointments together.
Guest	• Field Service Guest User License	Allows guest users with limited access for appointment booking and scheduling actions.

Note   Permission sets marked with an asterisk are not created in the newer Salesforce org; hence, they do not need to be assigned to the users.

To create permission sets, follow these steps:

1. Navigate to the App Launcher and select the Field Service admin app.

2. Click the Field Service Settings and then click Permissions Sets.

3. Click Create Permissions on each permission set.

4. Click Save (see Figure 3-4).

Figure 3-4. *Creating Field Service permission sets*

Once the permission is current, the Create Permissions link on the permission is replaced with a message stating that the permission set is up-to-date.

Assign users the permissions they require to execute their field service responsibilities after creating your field service permission sets.

To assign permission sets from the setup, follow these steps:

1. Navigate to Setup, and in the Quick Find box, enter
    Users. Then select Users.

2. Click the user's name you want to assign the
    permission sets for.

3. At the top of the page, click Permission Set
    Assignments.

4. Alternatively, scroll down to the Permission Set
    Assignments–related list.

5. Click Edit Assignments.

6. Assign the appropriate permission sets to the user
    and click Save.

Figure 3-5 shows an example of all the permissions assigned to a
mobile technician.

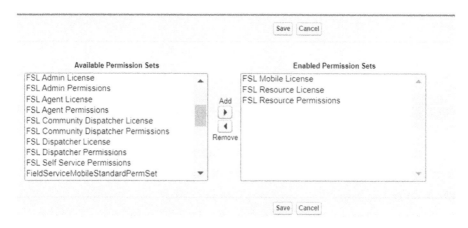

Figure 3-5. *Assigning permission sets to the user from setup*

While you can assign permissions from the setup, the recommended way to assign permissions to service resources is through the guided setup. You will learn to assign permissions and licenses to users using the guided setup in the "Using the Guided Setup" section of this chapter.

Assign Page Layouts

The Field Service managed package offers standard page layouts containing Visualforce components and Chatter actions. To use these page layouts, you need to assign them to profiles.

To assign page layouts, follow these steps:

1. Under Setup, search and navigate to Profiles.

2. Click the System Administrator profile.

3. Under the Page Layout section, search for Work Order and click View Assignment.

4. Click Edit Assignment.

5. Select all profiles and assign the Field Service Work Order layout.

6. Click Save (see Figure 3-6).

Figure 3-6. *Assigning page layouts*

7. Repeat the previous steps for the following objects:

- *Service Appointment*: Assign the FSL Service Appointment Layout.

- *Service Resource*: Assign the FSL Service Resource Layout.

- *Work Order Line Item*: Assign the FSL Work Order Line Item Layout.

- *Work Type*: Assign the FSL Work Type Layout.

- *Operating Hours*: Assign the FSL Operating Hours Layout.

You can assign page layouts to custom profiles as well.

Check for Data Integration Rules

Check that the data integration rules are current so that the service resource travel time is accurately calculated. When you add a street address to the following Field Service object records, Salesforce calculates the address's latitude, longitude, and location accuracy. This feature is called *geocoding*.

- Work orders

- Work order line items

- Service appointments

- Service territories

- Resource absences

- Service territory members

Data integration rules are used to keep the geocoding current. To check the data integration rules, do this:

1. Under Setup, search for and navigate to Data Integration Rules.

2. Click Geocodes for Work Order Address.

3. Ensure the rule is active.

4. Ensure all fields are checked except the Bypass Triggers field. Managed package triggers should be bypassed to calculate travel time accurately.

Repeat the steps for all other geocodes for the previously mentioned objects. To check the status of a record's geocoding data, navigate to the record and select Check for New Data in the action menu. For Salesforce Classic, add the Data Integration Rules–related list to the detail page layout of the records you want to track.

Geocode is refreshed when:

- The record is created or updated.

- The record type's data integration rule is deactivated and reactivated.

If you want to opt out of geocoding, deactivate the data integration rules. This will not calculate the travel time for service resources.

Using the Guided Setup

Thanks to the guided setup, admins can easily set up core elements of Field Service such as service territories, work types, skills, operating hours, service resources, dispatchers, and scheduling policies.

To access guided setup, follow these instructions:

1. Navigate to the App Launcher and select the Field Service admin app.

2. Click Field Service Settings.

3. On the Getting Started page, click Go to Guided Setup. Once you click Go to Guided Setup, you'll notice the system will check if you have the right permissions to access the guided setup. You should see warning messages if you're missing permissions (see Figure 3-7).

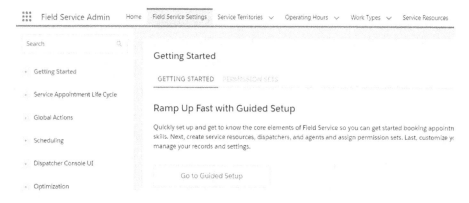

Figure 3-7. *Accessing the guided setup*

Figure 3-8 shows the guided setup. On the left side, you can see all the steps for setting up major parts of Field Service. The dashboard indicates all the records created. Admins can revisit the guided setup at any time to manage records and settings.

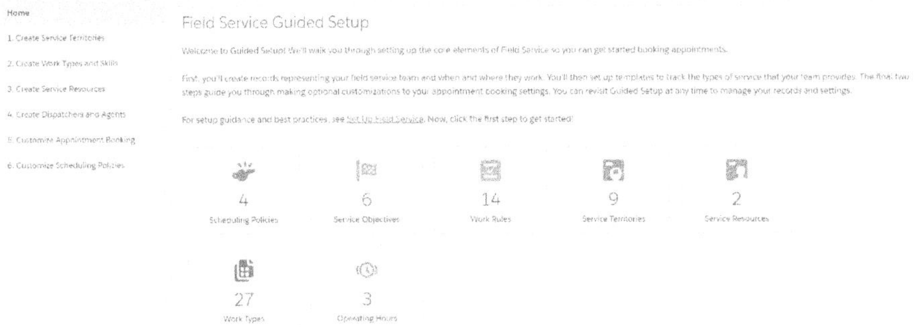

Figure 3-8. *Guided setup snapshot*

Follow the steps in the next section to configure the core elements of Field Service using the guided setup.

Setting Up Service Territories and Operating Hours

Service territories are geographic locations in which your team operates. Hierarchies of service territories can be created to organize the workforce and ensure that service resources are assigned to service appointments near their home location. Start by creating the highest level of territory and then create child territories depending on your business structure.

For example, you can create California as the highest level and then Northern California and Southern California as the second level, counties as the third level, cities as fourth level, and so on.

- California
  - Northern California
    - Alameda County
      - Oakland
      - Fremont

49

- Santa Clara County
  - San Jose
  - Palo Alto
- Southern California
  - Los Angeles County
    - Los Angeles
    - Santa Monica
  - Orange County
    - Newport Beach
    - Irvine

Service territories need not always represent geographic areas. In some cases, they can be used to group service resources into functional areas such as Sales, Service, or Marketing.

Important Tip   As a best practice, Salesforce recommends staying within the following limits:

Up to 50 service resources per service territory

Up to 1,000 service appointments per day per service territory

Up to 20 qualified service resources per service appointment

Operating hours are the working hours of the area's workforce. Unless otherwise specified on their service territory member records, territory residents use these hours (see Figure 3-9).

Figure 3-9. *Assigning service territories and operating hours*

To set up service territories and operating hours for your organization, follow these steps:

1. While on the guided setup, click Create Service Territories.

2. To create a service territory, enter the service territory name and click Add. To create a hierarchy, drag one territory on top of another.

3. To update additional fields on a service territory or attach files, select the territory name and click Open Service Territory Record.

4. To create operating hours, click the service territory, use the lookup to select existing operating hours, or click New Operating Hours to create your own.

5. For simplicity with appointment booking, always specify a time zone for your operating hours.

6. To create more complex time slots, save your new operating hours and click Open Operating Hours Record below the Operating Hours field. Navigate to the time slots–related lists and customize your time slots, as shown in Figure 3-10.

51

Operating Hours
PST Time

Time Zone
(GMT-07:00) Pacific Daylight Time (America/Los_Angeles)

Related   Details

Time Slots (6+)   New

Day of Week	Start Time	End Time	Type	
Monday	8:00:00 AM	1:00:00 PM	Normal	▼
Tuesday	8:00:00 AM	1:00:00 PM	Normal	▼
Wednesday	8:00:00 AM	1:00:00 PM	Normal	▼

Figure 3-10. Setting up time slots

Setting Up Work Types and Skills

Work types are templates that help you save time and standardize your
Field Service work. It's likely that your organization serves numerous
clients by performing the same operations repeatedly. You can create a
work type for each such operation and associate it to the work order. You
can also add skills required to complete a work type.

For example, work types for ABC Automobiles could be Recall, Oil, Filter
Change, Tire Rotation, Battery Performance Test, etc. (see Figure 3-11).

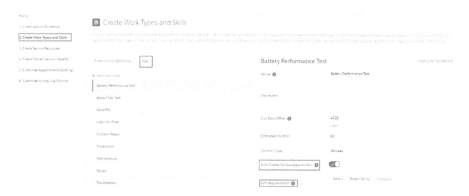

Figure 3-11. Creating work types and skills

To set up work types for your organization, follow these steps:

1. While on the Guided Setup screen, click the Create Work Types and Skills tab.

2. Enter a name and click Add to create a work type.

3. Update the Description, Due Date Offset, and Estimated Duration fields.

4. Select Auto-Create Service Appointment to automatically create service appointments on work orders or work order line items that use the work type.

Note   When a service appointment is autocreated, the due date is set to 7 days from the created date by default. This can be updated in the Field Service Settings from setup or by updating the Due Date Offset field on the specific work type.

---

5. Add any skills required to complete this work type under Skill Requirements.

Setting Up Service Resources

Service resources represent your workforce (see Figure 3-12).

Figure 3-12. *Creating service resources and assigning licenses*

To set up service resources, follow these steps:

1. While on the guided setup, click Create Service Resources.

2. Select User and then Service Territory and click Add.

3. Once the user is added, click the icons in the Licenses column to assign the Field Service Scheduling and Mobile licenses to service resources.

Just like you added skill requirements to the work type, you should add skills to the service resource. This allows the optimizer to match the skills on work type with the skills on service resources and choose the best skilled candidates for the job.

While working in the guided setup, select the service resource you want to assign the skills for and click the Update Skills button, as shown in Figure 3-13.

Figure 3-13. *Selecting a service resource for assigning skills*

Then select the skills you want to update and click Update Resource Skills, as shown in Figure 3-14.

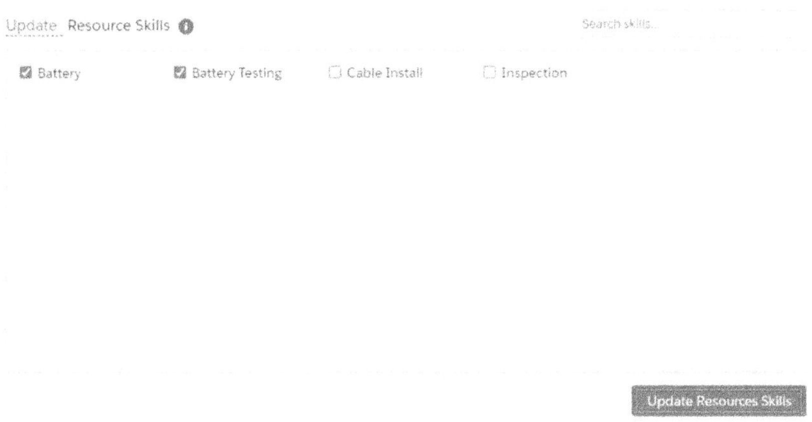

Update Resource Skills ⓘ   Search skills...

☑ Battery   ☑ Battery Testing   ☐ Cable Install   ☐ Inspection

Update Resources Skills

Figure 3-14. *Updating skills for service resources*

Alternatively, you can assign skills from the service resource record. While working in the guided setup, on the Service Resources tab, hover over a service resource name and click the Open Service Resource Record icon (see Figure 3-15).

☐ RESOURCE NAME ↑

☐ Amy Jackson

Figure 3-15. *Open Service Resource record*

Click the Related tab, navigate to the Service Resource Skill–related list, click New, and enter the skill, skill level, start date, and end date (if applicable) and save the record (see Figure 3-16).

Figure 3-16. *Creating the new service resource skill*

The skill level is used to measure the service resource's level of expertise for a particular skill. The skill level can range from 0 to 99.99. Scheduling considers the skill levels of your workforce to recommend most qualified candidates.

Setting Up Dispatchers and Agents

Similar to setting up service resources, to create dispatches and agents, follow these steps (see Figure 3-17).

Figure 3-17. *Creating dispatchers and agents*

1. Click Create Dispatchers and Agents.

2. Select a user and click Add.

3. Once the user is added, click the icons in the
    Licenses column to assign the Field Service
    Dispatcher or agent licenses and permissions to
    dispatchers or agents.

Customizing Appointment Booking

Salesforce Field Service offers the Book Appointment and Candidates
actions out of the box to schedule or reschedule service appointment slots
or look for candidates based on technician availability and arrival window
preference.

These actions can be added to service appointment, work order, work
order line items, work types, leads, assets, or opportunities page layouts
(see Figure 3-18).

Figure 3-18. *Customizing appointment booking*

To select the scheduling policy and operating hours, which will be used to optimize booking appointments and candidate actions, follow these steps:

1. Click Customize Appointment Booking from the guided setup.

2. Select the scheduling policy.

3. Select the operating hours.

Customizing Scheduling Policies

A scheduling policy is a collection of rules and objectives that directs the schedule optimizer's decisions. By default there are four scheduling policies to choose from, which are Customer First, Emergency, High Intensity, and Soft Boundaries. Your business can either use these policies or create a custom policy.

For example, you can create a policy that reduces the overall cost of logistics. You can also create custom work rules that will be added to the scheduling policy (see Figure 3-19).

Figure 3-19. *Customizing scheduling policies*

To create or update scheduling policy, follow these steps:

1. Click Customize Scheduling Policies from the guided setup.

2. Enter a name and click Add to create a new scheduling policy.

3. Select the name of the existing scheduling policy to update description, work rules, or service objective score.

Scheduling policies will be covered in greater detail in Chapter 4.

Creating Work Orders

Work orders are used to track the work for your team. Let's create work orders for ABC Automobiles (see Figure 3-20).

Figure 3-20. *Creating a new work order*

1. Navigate to the Work Orders tab from the App Launcher.

2. Click New (see Figure 3-21).

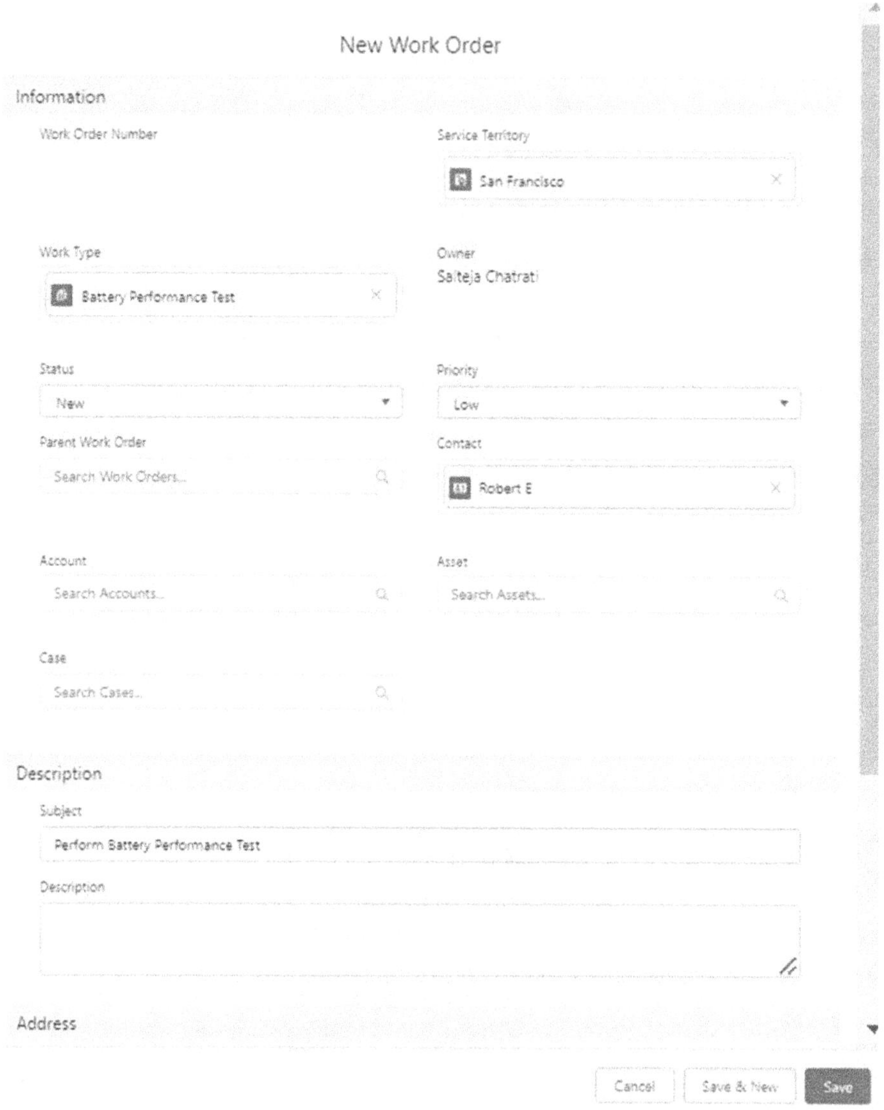

Figure 3-21. *Updating the work order details*

3. Select Work Type.

4. Enter other related information (if applicable) such
    as contact, account, asset, service territory, subject,
    description, and address. The work order's address
    is inherited by its service appointments and other
    line items.

5. Click Save.

Navigate to the Related tab to add the following details to the work
order. If you don't see a related list, you can add it to the work order page
layout. Go to Setup, navigate to the Object Manager tab, search for the
Work Order object, and navigate to the page layout. Under Related Lists,
drag and drop the related list and click Save.

- *Work order line item*: Create a work order line item if
  the work order has subtasks or steps to complete it.
  Each subtask can indicate a work order line item. For
  example, a work order for a multipoint car inspection
  may have work order line items for Inspect Headlights,
  Check Brake Fluid Level, Inspect Heat and Air
  Conditioning, etc.

- *Child work orders*: In situations when the work order is
  complex or large, you can create a child work order.

- *Service appointment*: Create service appointments to
  track scheduling details for the visits to the customers.

- *Skill requirements*: Add any skills that are required to
  complete the work order.

- *Articles*: These are relevant knowledge articles.

- *Resource preferences*: This is a service resource for the work order that's preferred, required, or excluded. Resource preference is set based on the resource preference on the work order's asset, location, or account, in that order. Salesforce sets the preference using the first resource preference it finds on an asset, then the location, and then the account. If a resource preference exists, Salesforce doesn't create a new one.

Note   When you add work type to the work order, it will autopopulate the following for the work order:

Duration

Duration type

Minimum crew size

Recommended crew size

Service report template

Skill requirements

Products required

Autocreation of a service appointment

Attached knowledge articles

Alternatively, work orders can be created from related lists or actions. For example, you can add a work order–related list on the case, lead, or opportunity and create a work order from these objects.

Figure 3-22 is the snapshot of sample work orders created for ABC Automobiles.

Figure 3-22. *Work orders list view*

Since we have checked Auto-Create Service Appointment on the work type, service appointments will be automatically created for the work orders.

Summary

To summarize, Salesforce Field Service can be easily configured by following the steps outlined in this chapter.

- Ensure Field Service is enabled for your Salesforce environment.

- Install the Field Service managed package to open up access to the dispatcher console, scheduled optimization, custom objects, and guided setup.

- Assign the right licenses and permissions to the players involved in the field service process.

- Assign page layouts to the profiles so that all the Visualforce components and chatter actions offered by managed package are visible to the users.

- Ensure data integration rules are set up correctly so that travel time for service resources is calculated accurately based on the geolocation information.

- Use the guided setup to configure service territories, operating hours, work types, skills, workforce, customize appointment booking, and scheduling policies.

- Once the configuration is complete, create work orders to capture the work details.

The upcoming chapter will cover the fundamentals of scheduling and optimization in Salesforce Field Service.

CHAPTER 4

Scheduling and Optimization

Salesforce Field Service allows optimized scheduling that meets predefined business objectives and KPIs.

This chapter addresses the following topics:

- What is schedule optimization?

- How does optimization work?

- Scheduling policies: work rules and service objectives

- Setting up optimization

- Relevance groups

- Service appointment time attributes and life cycle

- Scheduling actions

By the end of this chapter, you should be able to comprehend the principles of Field Service scheduling and how the optimization engine works.

© Saiteja Chatrati 2023
S. Chatrati, *Salesforce Field Service*, https://doi.org/10.1007/978-1-4842-9517-5_4

What Is Schedule Optimization?

Manually creating an effective schedule for your teams and customers can be challenging. The optimization tool for Field Service performs the work for you by creating an ideal schedule based on your organization's objectives. Schedule optimization assists you in adhering to service-level agreements and minimizing travel time, overtime, expenditures, and no-shows by establishing an optimal schedule.

How Does the Optimization Engine Work?

Behind the scenes, the Field Service schedule optimizer executes what is called the ***scheduling policy***. The scheduling policy is a scenario-based combination of work rules and service objectives.

- **Work rules** are yes/no qualifiers, which helps in filtering candidates suitable for a service appointment.

- **Service objectives** are weighted objectives set by the organization to measure the success of their customer service and support operations.

Based on the selected scheduling policy, the optimization engine automatically assigns the best resource to the service appointment. See Figure 4-1.

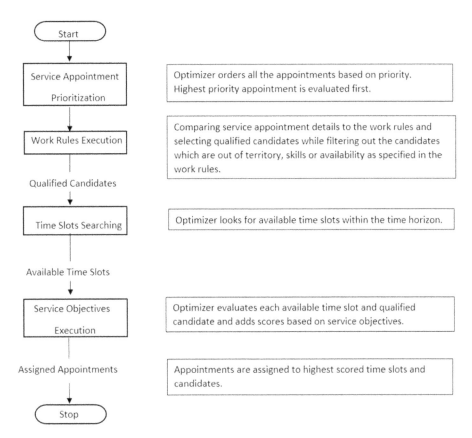

Figure 4-1. *Salesforce Field Service schedule optimization flow*

Based on all the relevant service appointments, service territories, and service resource data in a given time frame, the optimizer orders the appointments based on priority. Priority is specified based on the Work Order Priority, Work Order Line Item Priority, and Service Appointment Priority fields. The highest priority appointment is then evaluated first. Priority fields can be updated from the Field Service Admin app by going to Field Service Settings, then Scheduling, and then General Logic.

The optimization engine then compares the details of the prioritized appointment, such as the territory, necessary skills, and due date, to the work rules of the scheduling policy. Candidates who are ineligible are filtered out. The optimizer now has a pool of applicants who are qualified for the service appointment.

The optimization engine looks for available time slots within the time horizon between the earliest start time permissible for a service appointment and the due date or, if provided, the arrival window start and end dates.

The optimizer then evaluates each available time slot and qualified candidate and adds scores based on how fully the service objective is met. When the optimization is completed, it assigns the appointment to the candidate and time slot with the highest score.

The process of adding the scores and assigning the appointment with the highest score to the remaining candidates and time slots is repeated for all the service appointments sent for optimization. An overall utilization grade is received once the scheduling process is completed.

Scheduling Policies

Field Service offers four out-of-the-box scheduling policies, each of which is designed for a specific scenario (see Table 4-1).

Table 4-1. *List of Scheduling Policies*

Scheduling Policy	Description
Customer First	Provides excellent customer service while minimizing travel. The focus is to assign the customer's preferred resource and then to schedule the appointment as soon as possible. The second priority is to minimize travel.
High Intensity	This scheduled policy is preferred when there is a significant demand for services, such as during an earthquake or a storm. In this case, focus is to prioritize employee productivity over consumer preferences.
Soft Boundaries	Similar to the Customer First policy, but allowing service resources to be shared throughout territories for more service coverage.
Emergency	Used to dispatch appointments for emergency services. This is used with Emergency Chatter action.

Whenever you optimize your team's schedule, you can select a baseline scheduling policy. In most cases, the Customer First policy is recommended.

You can view existing or create new scheduling policies from the Scheduling Policies tab of the Field Service admin app. See Figure 4-2.

Figure 4-2. *Viewing or creating scheduling policies*

Work Rules

Work rules are rules defined by businesses that filter out resources not suitable for a service appointment by rejecting resources that do not match the rule. For example, if the Match Skill rule is selected, then the engine would assign service appointments to resources with matching skills only.

Work rules are driven by work rule types. **Work rule types** are record types for different work rules.

Table 4-2 lists all the work rule record types and standard work rules that are available out of the box.

Table 4-2. *Work Rule Record Types*

Work Rule Record Type	Description
Count Rule	This rule counts assignments, durations, or custom values to restrict appointment scheduling. This avoids overloading service resources.
Excluded Resources	A service resource won't be allocated to an appointment if their preference is listed as an excluded resource under the Excluded Resources work rule type.
	The following is a standard work rule of this type:
	• Excluded Resources: Selecting this work rule will ensure that specified excluded resources are excluded from scheduling.
Extended Match	This function compares a property from a service appointment object to a property listed in a service resource object.
Match Boolean	The Match Boolean work rule type uses a checkbox (Boolean) field on service resources to enforce scheduling preferences
	The following is a standard work rule of this type:
	• Active Resources: This work rule ensures that only active service resources are considered for scheduling.

(continued)

Table 4-2. (*continued*)

Work Rule Record Type	Description
Match Fields	A field on service appointments and a field on service resources are matched via the Match Fields work rule type.
Match Skills	Matches the required skills for a service appointment with the service resource's skills. If selected, service resources whose skill level is lower than the level specified on the Skill Requirement record for an appointment's parent record are not considered as candidates for appointment scheduling. The following is a standard work rule of this type: • Match Skills: When selected, the scheduling engine assigns service resources to the appointments based on matching skills.
Match Territory	This work rule type ensures that only service resources who are Primary or Relocation members of the appointment's service territory are assigned to service appointments. The following is a standard work rule of this type: • Match Territory: Ensures that the service resource is assigned based on home territory.

(*continued*)

Table 4-2. (*continued*)

Work Rule Record Type	Description
Match Time	Limits the scheduling window in accordance with the properties of the service appointment date and time. The following are standard work rules of this type: • Earliest Start Permitted: This work rule ensures that a service appointment's Scheduled Start is equal to or later than the Earliest Start Permitted. This is mandatory and is included in every standard scheduling policy. • Due Date:This work rule ensures a service appointment's Scheduled End is equal to or earlier than the Due Date. This is mandatory and is included in every standard scheduling policy. • Scheduled Start: This work rule ensures that a service appointment's Scheduled Start is equal to or later than the Arrival Window Start. • Scheduled End: This work rule ensures that a service appointment's Scheduled Start is equal to or earlier than the Arrival Window End. The time fields for service appointment are explained in the "Field Service Appointment Time Attributes and Life Cycle" section of this chapter.

(*continued*)

Table 4-2. (*continued*)

Work Rule Record Type	Description
Maximum Travel From Home	Limits the travel distance and time for service resources. The following is a standard work rule of this type: • Maximum Travel From Home: When selected, resources are scheduled based on the value specified in the Maximum Travel from Home field on the work rule. Units of measurement are determined by the value set in Maximum Travel from the Home Type field. For travel time, the unit is minutes, while for distance, the unit is miles or kilometers. The miles or kilometers preference is set in the Field Service admin app.
Required Resources	A Required Resources work rule type guarantees that the associated service appointments are allocated to a particular service resource if an account or work order specifies that resource as required The following is a standard work rule of this type: • Required Service Resource: If an account or work order specifies a resource as required, when selected, this work rule will ensure that the related service appointments are assigned to that resource.
Service Appointment Visiting Hours	Ensures that the service appointment is scheduled according to the customer's visiting hours. The following is a standard work rule of this type: • Service Appointment Visiting Hours: When selected, this rule ensures appointments are scheduled based on the operating hours specified for the account.

(*continued*)

Table 4-2. (*continued*)

Work Rule Record Type	Description
Service Crew Resource Availability	Service resource of type crew will be assigned to an appointment only if it meets the minimum crew size specified in the appointment's parent record. The following is a standard work rule of this type: • Service Crew Resource Availability: When selected, this rule will ensure appointments are assigned to the crew based on value specified in the Minimum Crew Size field on the work orders, work order line items, and work types.
Service Resource Availability	This rule ensures that service resources are available to schedule. Any short breaks or travel time in between service appointments is considered for scheduling. This type of work rule is necessary for any scheduling policy to ensure that scheduling respects resource absences. The following is a standard work rule of this type: • Service Resource Availability: When selected, this rule ensures service appointments are not assigned to service resources when they are not available. This rule considerstravel time, break times, service resource's operating hours, and the scheduled start and end time of other scheduled appointments.
TimeSlot Designated Work	Ensures that the service appointment can be scheduled only during the specified time slots.

(*continued*)

Table 4-2. (*continued*)

Work Rule Record Type	Description
Working Territories	Matches service resource working territories. By default, the Working Territories rule type matches only secondary territories. If you want the optimizer to consider the primary territory as well, select Working Location Enable Primary on the work rule.
	The following is a standard work rule of this type:
	• Working Territories: Ensures that service resources can move between service territories
	Both Working Territories and Match Territory cannot be included together in a scheduling policy. If your service resources work between primary and secondary territories, choose Working Territory work rule; otherwise, choose Match Territory work rule.

You can view existing or create new work rules from the Work Rules tab of the Field Service admin app. See Figure 4-3.

Figure 4-3. *Viewing or creating work rules*

Service Objectives

If one part of the scheduling policy is made up of work rules, the remaining is made of service objectives. **Service objectives** are goals set by business that should be met. For example, one of the business objectives could be to minimize travel time of the resources. In such cases, the Minimize Travel service objective may be selected.

Table 4-3 lists all the service objectives record types that are available out of the box.

Table 4-3. *Service Objective Record Types*

Service Objective Record Type	Description
ASAP	The objective is to schedule appointments as quickly as possible. This is to ensure customers receive prompt service. The soonest scheduling option is given a score of 100, while the latest is given a score of 0. The score is determined by an evaluation period of 0 to 30 days in the future if numerous appointments are to be scheduled.
Minimize Overtime	Evaluates the use of overtime. The score for this objective compares the n of overtime hours worked with the anticipated length of the service appointment. An hour-long appointment, for instance, receives a score of 0 if it is entirely scheduled during overtime. If there is a half-hour overtime, the score is 50.

(continued)

Table 4-3. (*continued*)

Service Objective Record Type	Description
Minimize Travel	Ensures the travel time is minimized. This objective score is calculated based on travel times. The score is measured for optimization operations and nonoptimization scheduling operations differently.
	For optimization operations such as global optimization, resource schedule optimization, in-day optimization, and the Reshuffle action, the travel time is assumed to be in the range of 0 to 120 minutes.
	For instance, an option with a travel time of 120 minutes receives a 0 score while, an option with 60 minutes travel time receives a score of 50. This range can be customized by Salesforce.
	For nonoptimization operations such as the Book Appointment, Candidates, Schedule, Fill-In Schedule, and Group Nearby Appointments actions, this objective's score is calculated according to the travel times available.
	Examples: • If the appointment is at the same site as the previous appointment, then the travel time would be zero minutes. In this case, the objective score will be 100. • If the appointment is at a site that is 30 minutes away from the previous appointment's site, then the objective score will be 50. • If the appointment is at a site that is 60 minutes away from the previous appointment's site, then the objective score will be zero.

(*continued*)

Table 4-3. (*continued*)

Service Objective Record Type	Description
Preferred Service Resource	This ensures the customer's preferred resource is scheduled. The objective receives a score of 100 if the appointment is assigned to the preferred resource as specified in the parent work order; otherwise, the score is zero.
Resource Priority	The objective score is calculated based on the *priority* field on service resource. The score of the objective increases as the resource priority decreases.
Skill Level	This ensures that assigned resources have the required skills as specified in the skill requirements for the work order. This objective lets you pick the least or most qualified candidate. • Least Qualified: Prefers resources with lowest skills but good enough to complete the task. For example, if the skill requirement is 65 for Speaking Spanish, then a resource with 70 is preferred over 90 in speaking Spanish. • Most Qualified: Prefers resources with highest skills. For example, if the skill requirement is 65 for Speaking Spanish, then a resource with 90 is preferred over 70 in speaking Spanish.

You can view existing or create new service objectives from the Service Objectives tab of the Field Service admin app. See Figure 4-4.

Figure 4-4. *Viewing or creating service objectives*

Adding Work Rules and Service Objectives to the Scheduling Policy

Work rules and service objectives can be added to the scheduling policies from the Customize Scheduling Policies page in the guided setup.

Navigate to the Field Service admin app, and then go to the Field Service Settings. Click Go to Guided Setup, click Customize Scheduling Policies, and select the Scheduling Policy. See Figure 4-5.

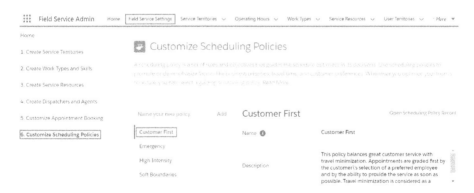

Figure 4-5. *Customizing scheduling policy using the guided setup*

To add work rules, while in the scheduling policy, under the Available Work Rules column, select the work rule and move it to the Selected Work Rules column, as shown in Figure 4-6.

Figure 4-6. Adding work rules using the guided setup

To add service objectives, for each service objective assign a weight indicating its importance, as shown in Figure 4-7.

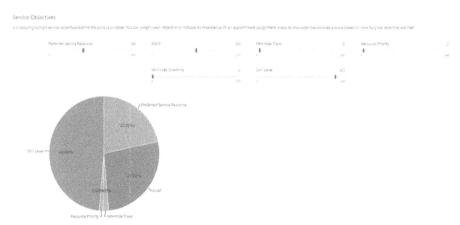

Figure 4-7. Adding service objectives using the guided setup

Schedule Optimization Key Pointers

The following are some tips:

- Optimization can move appointments that were previously scheduled when it finds a slot with a better grade or when it tries to fix an overlap.

- If an optimization unschedules an appointment and can't find another suitable slot, the appointment remains unscheduled after the optimization is completed.

- The optimizer considers scheduled service appointments that have already begun (the scheduled start time is in the past) as pinned and does not change or reschedule them.

- When optimizing your team's or a service resource's schedule, appointments with rule violations remain pinned. When the service appointment doesn't adhere to the scheduling guidelines in the scheduling policy you've chosen, a rule violation occurs. For instance, scheduling an appointment before the earliest permitted start date or assigning it to a resource who lacks a necessary skill both violate the rules.

- With enhanced scheduling and optimization, the optimization engine tries to fix rule violations to improve the schedule by rescheduling or unscheduling rule-violating appointments. To keep these appointments scheduled as is on the Gantt chart, the service appointments must first be pinned or in a pinned status.

Optimization Options

The Salesforce Field Service managed package provides several optimization options that determine whether the schedule of a single resource or the schedule of a whole service territory is included in the scope of optimization.

- *Global optimization*: Global optimization is the most extensive and effective optimization and takes the longest to execute. This optimizes your team's schedule for one or more territories within a specified range of days. You can set up this optimization frequently.

- *In-day optimization*: On the day of service, quickly optimize your team's schedule for one or more service territories to avoid last-minute scheduling hiccups.

- *Resource optimization*: On the day of the service, an individual service resource's schedule is optimized.

Set Up Optimization

Set up optimization to make appointments and handle last-minute problems. You can schedule optimization to perform automatically or manually.

Create the Field Service Optimization Profile and User

Follow these steps:

1. Navigate to the App Launcher and select the Field Service admin app.

2. Click Field Service Settings.

3. Click Optimization.

4. Click Activation.

5. Click Create Optimization Profile. On creation, a dialog prompt appears specifying the following:

    - There's a new optimization user.

    - The Field Service Optimization profile is assigned to it.

    - You want to switch to the new Field Service Optimization user.

6. Click OK.

Authorize the Field Service Optimization User

Search for the Field Service Optimization user and authorize it by following these steps:

1. From Setup, in the Quick Find box, enter **users**.

2. On the Users tab, click letter F to search for the Field Service Optimization user.

3. Note the username and click Edit next to the user.

4. Enter your email address and select Active.

5. Scroll down to select "Generate new password and notify user immediately."

6. Verify your email and click Save. See Figure 4-8.

Action	Full Name ↑	Alias	Username	Role	Active	Profile
☐ Edit	Field Service Optimization	optUsr	fs.00d5y000002tkj0uak.0ogovtmfpvek.8zn6nnv77fgo@fieldservice.com		✓	Field Service Optimization

Figure 4-8. *Authorizing the Field Service Optimization user*

Open the new password email that you received for the Field Service Optimization user.

7. In the password email, click Verify Account to set up a new password.

8. Enter new password details and click "Change password."

Activate Optimization

Follow these steps:

1. While logged in, navigate to the App Launcher and select the Field Service admin app.

2. Click Field Service Settings.

3. Click Optimization.

4. Click Activation.

Note Once the Field Service Optimization profile is created with required permissions, do not edit it.

Like all users, the Field Service Optimization user will require a license.

Monitor Optimization Requests

To monitor optimization requests, create a custom tab for the Optimization Request object by going to Setup, Tabs, Custom Object Tabs, and New. Customize the list view to show useful fields such as Status, Start, Finish, Type, Result, and Failure Reason. Once created, navigate to the tab and click any request to view its details. See Figure 4-9.

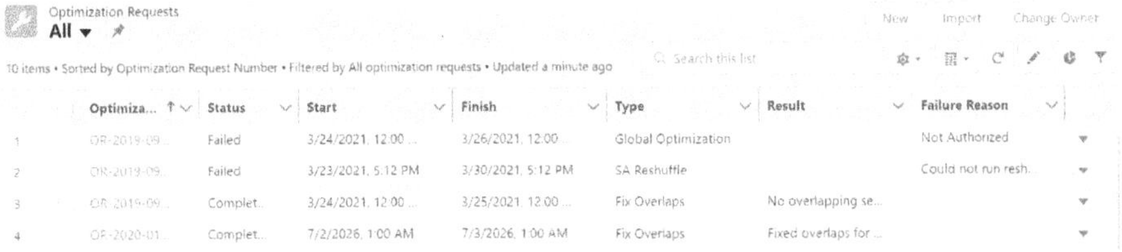

Figure 4-9. *Optimization requests*

Alternatively, you can view optimizations on the dispatcher console's Gantt chart.

Relevance Groups

A **relevance group** is a group of service appointments or service territory members who need their own set of work rules and service objectives.

For example, if you want to use the Maximum travel from Home work rule differently for full-time and part-time workers, create two work rules, one for full-time and one for part-time, and add the relevance group Visualforce page to the page layout of work rule to select the service appointments and service territory members who will be using the rule.

To add a relevance group to a work rule or service objective page layout, follow these steps (see Figure 4-10):

1. Navigate to Object Manager, Work Rule or Service Objective, and then Page Layout.

2. Click Visualforce Pages.

3. Drag and drop the following Visualforce pages for work rules and service objectives:

    Work Rule: Vf001GroupOnWorkRules

    Service Objective: Vf002GroupOnObjectives

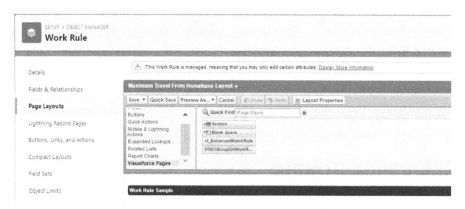

Figure 4-10. *Adding a relevance group Visualforce page to the page layout*

4. Once the relevance group is added to the page, you can specify the service territory members and service appointments using this work rule. Figure 4-11 shows the relevance group when added to the page layout.

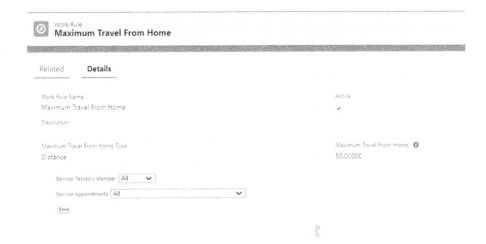

Figure 4-11. *Relevance group*

Service Appointment Time Attributes and Life Cycle

Service appointment records hold time fields that are taken into consideration during schedule optimization. These fields include the following:

- *Earliest Start Date*: The time frame by which the appointment needs to be finished.

- *Due Date*: The deadline for finishing the appointment. The Due Date and Earliest Start Permitted fields often correspond to provisions in the service-level agreement with the customer.

- *Arrival Window Start and Arrival Window End*: The start and end of the time window within which the resource is expected to arrive at the location. To account for delays and schedule changes, this window is often bigger than the scheduled start and end windows.

- *Scheduled Start and Scheduled End*: The time the appointment is supposed to begin and end. When the appointment is allocated to a resource in the Field Service managed package using the scheduling optimizer, these fields are filled in. See Figure 4-12.

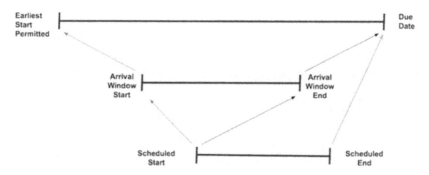

Figure 4-12. *Service appointment time attributes(Source: developer. salesforce.com)*

The service appointment life cycle refers to the various stages involved in managing and completing a service appointment. The following are statuses for service appointments corresponding to different stages in their life cycles:

- *None*: A new service appointment is created, either manually by a dispatcher or agent or automatically via a work order, work order line item, or other trigger.

- *Scheduled*: The job is scheduled to an available service resource, based on criteria such as location, skill set, and availability.

- *Dispatched*: The scheduled appointment details are sent to the service resource, either via email, via text message, or within the Salesforce Field Service mobile app.

- *In Progress*: The service resource arrives at the field site and checks in using the Salesforce Field Service mobile app. This triggers the start of the appointment.

- *Completed*: The service resource completes the work required for the appointment, using the tools and resources available in the Salesforce Field Service mobile app.

- *Cannot Complete*: The service resource is unable to complete the work.

- *Canceled*: The service appointment is canceled.

You can update the names of the statuses from the Status picklist field from the Service Appointment object in the setup.

Changing the name doesn't change a status's automatic transition behavior. You can customize the service appointment life cycle according to your business needs.

1. Navigate to the App Launcher and select the Field Service admin app.

2. Click Field Service Settings.

3. Click Service Appointment Life Cycle.

4. Click SA Status and select a status value for each description. Click Save. See Figure 4-13.

Figure 4-13. *Customizing the service appointment statuses*

5. Click the Status Transitions tab.

6. Each row indicates a flow or transition in the service appointment life cycle. Modify the existing flows, delete flows, or add new ones. Optionally, to restrict which user profiles can change each status, click More Details. Also, you can decide which specific Visualforce page should be shown whenever a user wants to update the status. Status flows are depicted in the status flow diagram; however, restrictions based on profiles are not shown. See Figure 4-14.

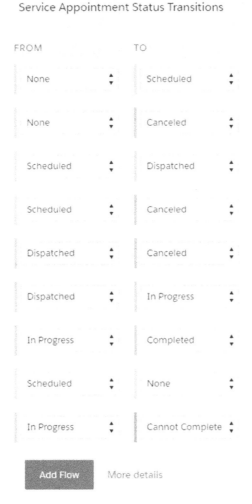

Figure 4-14. *Customizing service appointment transitions*

Note   An unscheduled service appointment status becomes None.

Emergency service appointments do not take status transitions into consideration when they are dispatched.

Using Scheduling Actions

Salesforce Field Service offers built-in actions to schedule appointments. The Book Appointment and Candidate actions in Salesforce Field Service enables support agents or customers to schedule and create a new appointment. Customers can use the Book Appointment action if it is embedded in the experience builder site. These actions allow scheduling appointments from a work order, work order line item, account, asset, lead, opportunity, or service appointment record itself.

To schedule an appointment using the Book Appointment or Candidate actions, ensure that these actions are added to the page layout of the record from where you want to schedule an appointment (for example, work order or service appointment record).

To schedule an appointment using the Book Appointment action from work order, do the following:

1. Navigate to the work order record and click Book Appointment action from the chatter feed.

2. Enter all the information and click Get Appointments. See Figure 4-15.

Figure 4-15. *Getting appointment slots: Book Appointment action*

3. To schedule an appointment, click any of the appointment slots. See Figure 4-16.

Figure 4-16. *Selecting an appointment slot, Book Appointment action*

Once you select the slot, you should see confirmation for the scheduled appointment. Click View Service Appointment for details. The scheduled appointment will also be visible in the dispatcher console for the specified date/time.

To search for ideal candidates in a specific territory, use the Candidates action.

1. Navigate to the record and click Candidates action from the chatter feed.

2. Enter the territory and click Get Candidates. See Figure 4-17.

Figure 4-17. *Getting candidates, Candidates action*

3. You should see all the candidates available for the specified territory. See Figure 4-18.

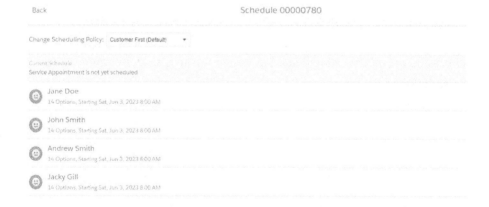

Figure 4-18. *Selecting a candidate, Candidates action*

4. Select a candidate to see available slots and the grade for each slot. Select a slot and schedule an appointment for the candidate.

You can manage these actions from the Field Service admin app. Go to Field Service Settings, click Global Actions, and click Appointment Booking.

Important Tip   If you see "No slots were found" or "No candidates were found" warning while using the previous scheduling actions, confirm that the service appointment related to the work order or work order line item has no violations. You can check the rule violations from the Gantt chart in the dispatcher console.

Summary

In this chapter, you learned the following:

- In Salesforce Field Service, the term *schedule optimization* refers to the process of developing effective schedules for field service personnel to increase productivity and save travel time and expenses.

- The optimizer uses scheduling policies as guidelines to schedule appointments. Scheduling policies are a combination of work rules and service objectives.

- Work rules are yes/no qualifiers, which help in refining candidates suitable for a service appointment.

- Service objectives are weighted objectives set by the organization that represent the scheduling policy's purpose. These objectives are typically related to customer satisfaction, service-level agreements, and other key performance indicators.

- The optimizer first filters all the qualified candidates based on the work rules and then selects the highest scored candidates out of all the qualified candidates according to the service objectives.

- Field Service provides Global, In-Day, and Resource optimization options that determine whether the schedule of a single resource or the schedule of a whole service territory is included in the scope of optimization.

- To activate optimization, first create a Field Service Optimization profile with the required permissions and then authorize the Field Service user.

- Relevance groups can be used to manage groups of service appointments or service territory members having their own set of work rules or service objectives.

- The service appointment life cycle involves various stages from start to completion. You can customize these stages according to your business needs.

- Built-in global actions like Book Appointment and Candidates can be used to create and schedule service appointments.

In the next chapter, you will learn about some of the additional Field Service capabilities offered by Salesforce.

CHAPTER 5

Managing Field Service Capabilities

In the previous chapters, you learned how to set up Salesforce Field Service for your business. In this chapter, you will understand how to leverage some of the important capabilities offered by Salesforce in detail. This chapter will also cover the dispatcher console, which helps dispatchers efficiently track their service appointments and workforce.

On a high level, the topics covered in this chapter include the following:

- Managing service resources

- Preventive maintenance

- Managing service reports

- Using the dispatcher console

Managing Service Resources

Service resources are professionals who will be performing the actual field service jobs. Salesforce offers various features to help service resources log their timesheets, indicate their absences, work as a team, check out their appointments in a calendar, and track their travel routes beforehand. Let's understand these capabilities in detail.

© Saiteja Chatrati 2023

S. Chatrati, *Salesforce Field Service*, https://doi.org/10.1007/978-1-4842-9517-5_5

Logging Timesheets

Service resources can use the Field Service application on their mobile devices to log timesheets for tracking their time and work. Timesheets can be set up in four easy steps, as shown here:

1. Enable mobile timesheets.

2. Create an approval process to send the timesheet submitted by the service resource for manager approval.

3. Add or remove any fields for timesheets that you want to display on the Field Service mobile app.

4. Create timesheet templates if you want to automatically create timesheets.

Let's look at these in more detail. To enable mobile timesheets, follow these steps:

1. From the setup, in the Quick Find box, search and select Field Service Mobile Settings.

2. Click the drop-down list next to Field Service Mobile Settings and click Show Details. For older versions, click Edit.

3. In the Additional Settings section, select the Enable Mobile Timesheets checkbox and click Save. See Figure 5-1.

Figure 5-1. *Enabling mobile timesheets*

To create an approval process, follow these steps:

1.   From the setup, in the Quick Find box, search and
     select Approval Processes.

2.   Under Manage Approval Processes For, select
     "Time sheet."

3.   Click Create New Approval Process and Use Jump
     Start Wizard. See Figure 5-2.

Figure 5-2. *Creating an approval process*

4. Enter the approval process name.

5. Specify the criteria when the approval process should trigger. For example, you can trigger the approval process when the status of the timesheet is Submitted.

6. Select the approver.

7. Click Save. See Figure 5-3.

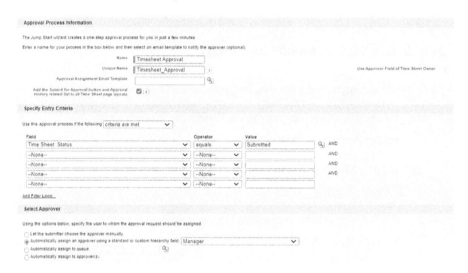

Figure 5-3. *Timesheet approval process*

Activate the approval process. Optionally, you can set up actions for initial submission, approval steps, final approval, final rejection, and recall from the approval process detail page.

To customize the fields for timesheets, follow these steps:

1. From the setup, navigate to the Object Manager tab, search for the Time Sheet object, and click it.

2. Navigate to the page layout.

3. Under Fields, drag and drop all the fields you want to display. Up to four fields can be shown on the Field Service mobile app.

4. Under Related Lists, if not already added, drag and drop the lists related to Approval History and Time Sheet Entries.

5. Click Save. See Figure 5-4.

Figure 5-4. *Customizing the timesheet fields*

To set up the timesheet templates, first create a timesheet template and then assign the template to the user profiles.

To create a new timesheet template, follow these steps:

a. From Setup, in the Quick Find box, search and select Time Sheet Settings.

b. Click New.

c. Fill in all the following information:

  • *Name*: Label of the template.

- *Developer Name*: API name that uses underscores instead of spaces.

- *Start Date*: Date when the timesheet template should be applied. Because the timesheet autocreation job runs once per day, set a start date that is at least 24 hours in the future.

- *Frequency*: Frequency when the new timesheets are automatically created. For instance, if you select the "weekly" frequency option, a new timesheet will be created every week, beginning on the start date you provided and covering the entire week.

- *Workweek Start and End days*: Days when the week begins and ends. For example, Monday to Friday.

- *Description*: Description of the template.

d. Select the Active checkbox and click Save. See Figure 5-5.

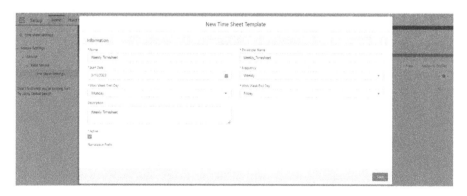

Figure 5-5. *Creating a timesheet template*

To assign this template to the user profiles, click Assign to Profiles next to the New button. Select the profiles and click Change Assignments. As shown in Figure 5-6, select the timesheet template you just created under Time Sheet Setting and click Save.

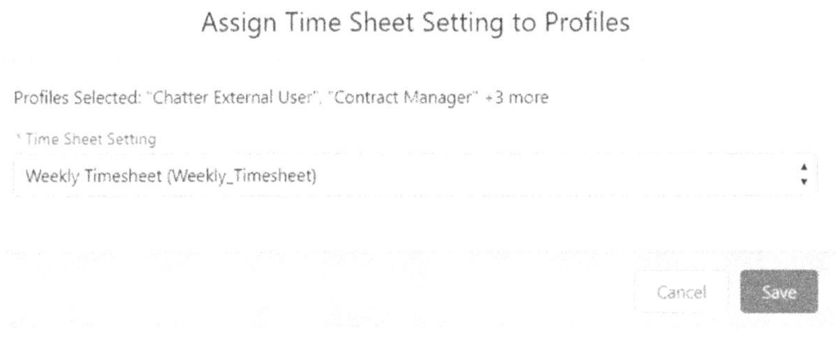

Assign Time Sheet Setting to Profiles

Profiles Selected: "Chatter External User", "Contract Manager" +3 more

* Time Sheet Setting

Weekly Timesheet (Weekly_Timesheet)

Cancel   Save

Figure 5-6. *Assigning a timesheet template to user profiles*

Note   You can check if the timesheets are autocreated by creating a list view or report on the timesheet object. If the autocreation process can't create a timesheet, it doesn't retry.

You can also create timesheets manually from the service resource record. If not already added, add the timesheets-related list to the service resource page layout. From the setup, navigate to the Object Manager tab, search for the Service Resource object, and navigate to the page layout. If it's not already added, add the timesheets-related list to the page layout.

Navigate to the service resource record and click the Related tab. From the timesheets-related list, click New, as shown in Figure 5-7.

Figure 5-7. *Timesheets-related list*

Specify the timesheet start and end dates and save the timesheet. Timesheets can be created for service resources of type Technician only. See Figure 5-8.

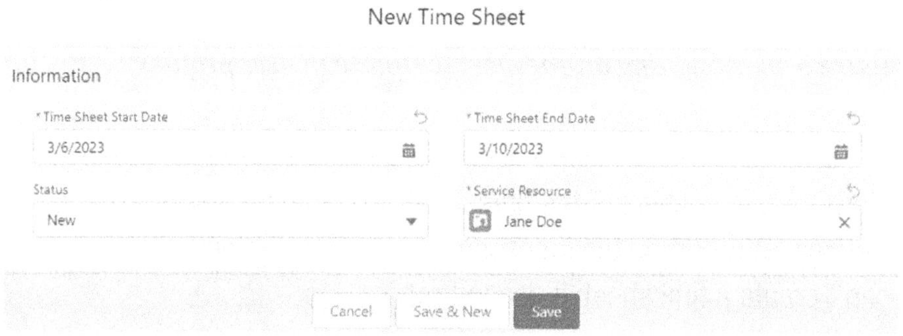

Figure 5-8. *Creating a new timesheet*

Timesheets are composed of timesheet entries. Timesheet entries typically track individual tasks such as travel or asset repair. Once you have created a timesheet, create a single timesheet entry for each task. Navigate to the timesheet entries–related list from the Related tab of the timesheet you just created and click New. Enter the start and end date/time, subject, description, and work order or work order line item for which the time sheet entry is created and save the timesheet entry. See Figure 5-9.

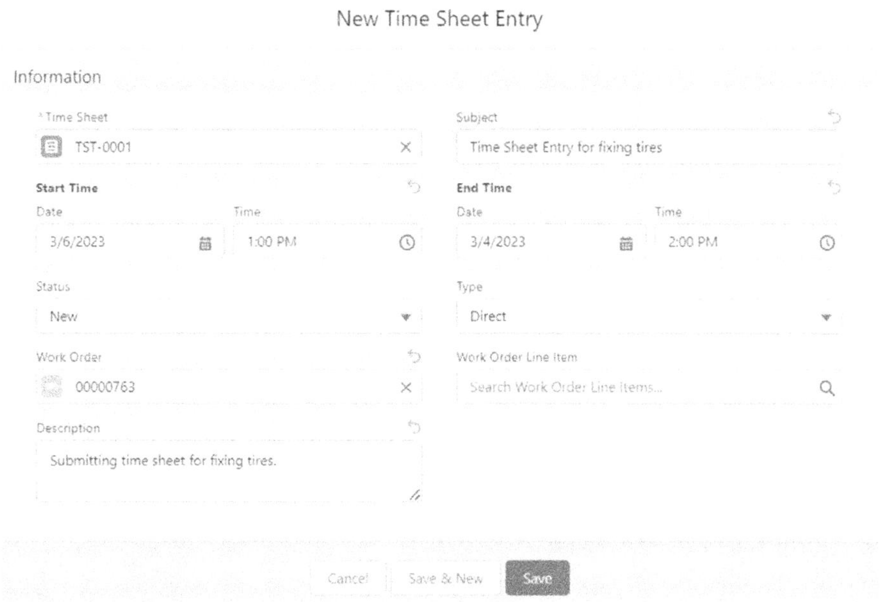

New Time Sheet Entry

Information

| Time Sheet | | Subject |
| TST-0001 | ✕ | Time Sheet Entry for fixing tires |

Start Time

Date	Time		**End Time**	
3/6/2023	1:00 PM		Date	Time
			3/4/2023	2:00 PM

| Status | | Type |
| New | ▼ | Direct |

| Work Order | | Work Order Line Item |
| 00000763 | ✕ | Search Work Order Line Items... |

Description

Submitting time sheet for fixing tires.

Cancel   Save & New   **Save**

Figure 5-9. *Creating a new timesheet entry*

You can track the number of timesheet entries linked to the timesheet from the Time Sheet Entry Count field on the timesheet. See Figure 5-10.

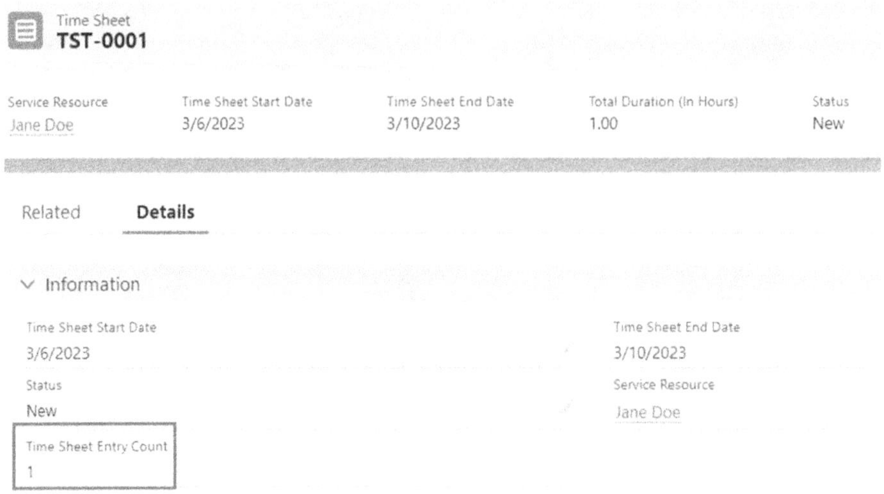

Figure 5-10. *Timesheet entry count*

Note   Salesforce has some recommendations for timesheets.

If you add a required custom field that uses custom values, timesheets aren't automatically created.

Using the same workweek start day and workweek end day results in a workweek that is one day long.

Twice a month frequency uses days 1–15 as the first half of the month and days 16–31 as the second half of the month.

Start date defines the day your time sheet begins. So if your time sheet template's start date is on a Tuesday, your workweek start day is Monday, and if you set the frequency to every two weeks, the first time sheet starts on Tuesday. The time sheet autocreation job creates the first batch of timesheets when it runs on Monday. Thereafter, timesheets start on Mondays, and they are automatically created when the job runs on Sundays.

Timesheet templates aren't included in updates to the managed package.

Learn how mobile users can submit timesheets from the Field Service mobile app in Chapter 7.

Creating Service Crews

A service crew is a group of resources who work together to complete a specific task. For example, in a car service center, a service request may require a group of technicians with expertise in both interiors and exteriors.

You can create service crews in two ways.

- Using the Service Crews tab in the app launcher

- Using the Crew Management Tool

To create service crews from the Service Crews tab in the app launcher, follow these steps:

1. Navigate to the Service Crews tab and click New.

2. Enter the service crew name and crew size and click Save.

3. To add members to the crew, navigate to the related tab, under the Service Crew Members–related list, click New.

4. Enter the start and end date/time.

5. Select a service resource.

6. Select Leader if the member is leading the crew.

7. Click Save & New if you want to add more members; otherwise, click Save. See Figure 5-11.

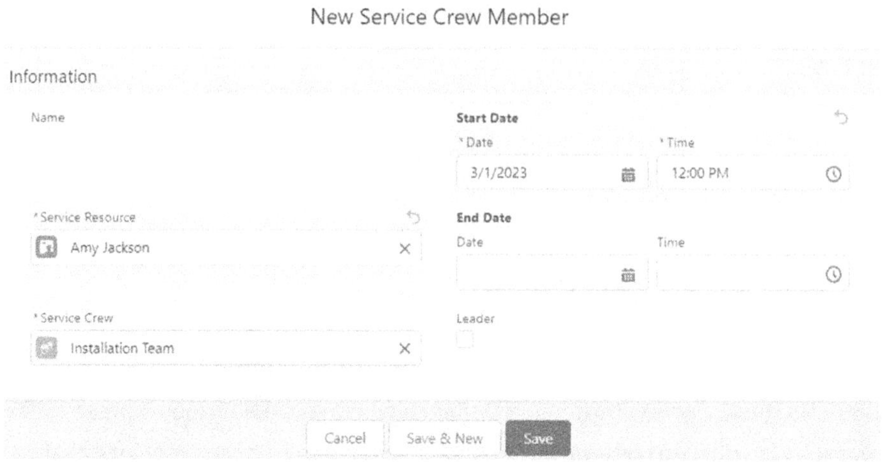

New Service Crew Member

Information

Name

Start Date

* Date

3/1/2023

* Time

12:00 PM

* Service Resource

Amy Jackson

End Date

Date

Time

* Service Crew

Installation Team

Leader

Cancel   Save & New   Save

Figure 5-11. *Creating a new service crew using the Service Crews tab*

If you want to schedule appointments for the service crew, create a service resource of type Crew and link it to the service crew. If it's not already added, add the Service Crew field to the service resources page layout from the setup.

1. Navigate to the Service Resources tab and click New.

2. Enter the service resource name.

3. Leave the user field blank and specify the crew in the Service Crew field, as shown in Figure 5-12.

4. Select the Active checkbox and save the record.

Figure 5-12. *Creating a service resource for the crew*

As an admin, you can set up the Crew Management Tool that comes with the managed package to help dispatchers or managers manage their crews efficiently. To set up the Crew Management Tool, follow these steps:

1. Decide which users need access to the Crew Management Tool and assign them at least one of these permission sets:

   • FSL Admin Permissions

   • FSL Dispatcher Permissions

2. Create a Crew Management tab in one of
    these ways:

    •   Create a Visualforce page named Crew
        Management for the FSL.CrewManagement page.

    •   Embed the Crew Management custom Lightning
        component in a Lightning page.

    Let's see how to create the Crew Management tab
    using the Visualforce page.

    a. As shown in Figure 5-13, from the setup, in the Quick Find
        box, search for and select Tabs.

    b. In the Visualforce Tabs section, click New.

    c. Select the CrewManagement Visualforce page.

    d. Enter the label, description, and tab style, and click Next.

    e. Add the tab to profiles and custom apps and click Save.

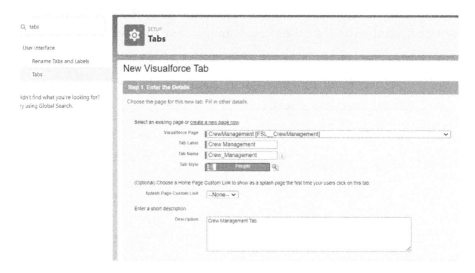

Figure 5-13. *Creating the Visualforce Crew Management tab*

3. Create a new permission set with access to the
    following and assign it to the relevant users:

    • Crew Management tab

    • FSL.CrewManagement Apex class

    • Visualforce pages:

        • FSL.CrewManagement Visualforce page

        • FSL.CrewsResourceLightbox Visualforce page

        • FSL.CrewsSaLightbox Visualforce page

        • FSL.CrewsWorkorderLightbox Visualforce page

        • FSL.CrewsWorkorderLineItemLightbox
          Visualforce page

Figure 5-14 shows an example of the crew management permission
sets with Visualforce pages assigned.

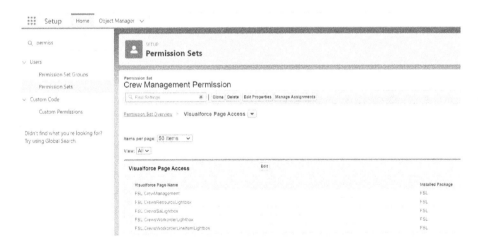

Figure 5-14. *Crew management permission sets with*
Visualforce pages

As a dispatcher or crew manager, if you have the right permissions assigned, you can use the Crew Management Tool to create and manage service crews. As shown in Figure 5-15, open the tool by navigating to the app launcher and searching for the Crew Management tab. To create a service crew, select a service territory and click New Service Crew.

Figure 5-15. *Creating a new service crew using the Crew Management Tool*

1. Under Basics, fill in the Crew Name and Gantt Label fields. Click Next.

2. Assign skills to the crew if any.

3. Select the crew leader or manager and click Save. See Figure 5-16.

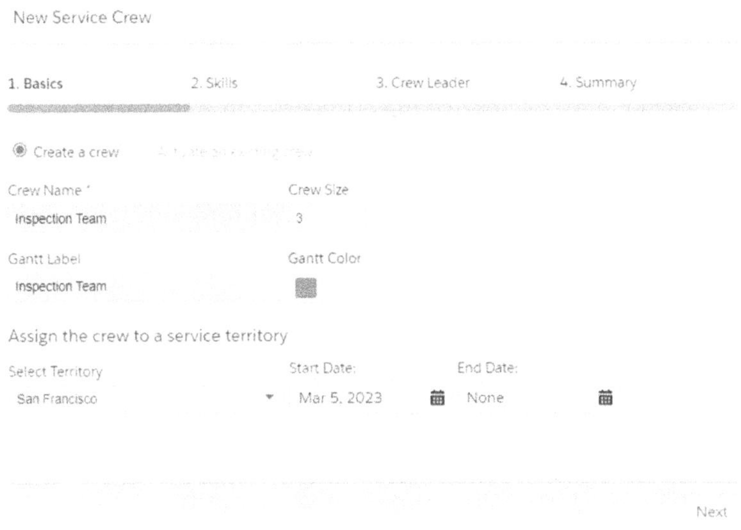

New Service Crew

1. Basics   2. Skills   3. Crew Leader   4. Summary

⦿ Create a crew

Crew Name *   Crew Size
  Inspection Team   3

Gantt Label   Gantt Color
  Inspection Team   ▨

Assign the crew to a service territory

Select Territory   Start Date: End Date:
  San Francisco   ▾   Mar 5, 2023   📅   None   📅

                                                                    Next

Figure 5-16. *Service crew details*

The service crews will be displayed on the dispatcher console under the specified service territory.

Creating Resource Absences

Many times service resources may not be available for work. You can track resource absences from the Absences-related list on the service resource records. During schedule optimization, service resources aren't assigned to appointments that conflict with their absences. If not already added, add the Absences-related list to the service resource page layout from the setup.

As shown in Figure 5-17, to add an absence record for a resource, follow these steps:

1. Navigate to the Service Resources tab from the app launcher.

2. From the Service Resources tab, navigate to the resource record you want to track absence for.

3. Navigate to the Related tab and to the Absences-related list.

4. Click New Recurring Absences, if you want to create a series of regularly scheduled absences. Click New, if you want to create a single absence record.

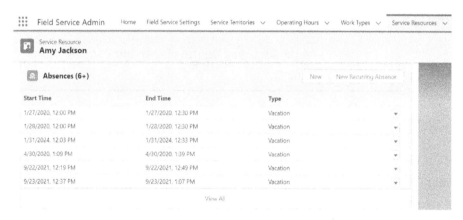

Figure 5-17. *Service resource absences-related list*

Fill in the fields as shown in Figure 5-18.

5. In the record type field, select Non-Availability. The Break record type is used to automatically create breaks during schedule optimization.

6. Select an absence type. You can add more absence types by updating the Type picklist field on the resource absence object in the setup.

7. Enter the start time and end time.

8. For the recurring absence record, specify the recurrence period, frequency, and recurrence end. If you have entered a weekly recurrence period and frequency of 2, then the resource absence occurs every 2 weeks until the recurrence ends as specified.

9. Enter an address if applicable. For example, enter the location where the training is conducted. This address is used to determine the travel time to and from adjacent service appointments. Appointments aren't scheduled during the dedicated travel time. If the address is not provided, the resource's home base is used to calculate the travel time to the next service appointment.

10. Enter the Gantt label to indicate how the absence appears in the Gantt chart. Gantt labels aren't available on the Break and Recurring absence types.

11. Enter a description and click Save.

New Recurring Absence

Information

* Resource

🔲 Jacky Gill   ×

* Record Type

Non Availability   ▼

* Type

Training   ▼

Start Time   **End Time**

* Date   * Time   * Date   * Time

Mar 15, 2023   📅 | 9:00 AM   🕐   Mar 15, 2023   📅 | 11:00 AM   🕐

Recurrence Pattern

* Recurrence Period   * Frequency ⓘ   * Recurrence Days

Weeks   ▼ | 1   Sun   Mon   Tue   **Wed**   Thu   Fri   Sat

* Recurrence End

● After Occurrences

| 2 |

○ Date

| 📅 |

Details

Address

Address

| Palo Alto St |
| ⁄⁄ |

City   State/Province

| Palo Alto | | CA |

Zip/Postal Code   Country

Figure 5-18. Creating a recurring absence record

Note   If a service resource of type Crew has resource absences, those absences are considered in scheduling and shown on the Gantt chart, while absences associated with individual crew members' corresponding service resources aren't considered for scheduling.

In Chapter 7, you will learn how mobile users can add resource absences from the Field Service mobile app.

Preventive Maintenance

Preventive maintenance is a maintenance that is regularly performed on the assets to reduce the risk of equipment failure and unplanned machine downtime. In Salesforce, assets are referred to as *products* that are purchased or installed by the customer. You can create preventive maintenance plans for assets so your customers are always on time. Once you set up a maintenance schedule, work orders will be generated according to the schedule.

Follow this four-step process to set up a maintenance schedule for assets:

1. Create a maintenance plan to track the information of the maintenance schedule.

2. Create a maintenance work rule to specify the entry criteria for the maintenance plan.

3. Create a maintenance asset to associate assets to the maintenance plan. Assets are goods or services purchased or installed by the customer.

4. Generate work orders for maintenance plans.

Maintenance Plans

Using maintenance plans, you can mass-generate work orders for upcoming visits and specify how frequently maintenance visits take place. To create a maintenance plan, from the app launcher, search for the Maintenance Plans tab. From the Maintenance Plans tab, click New, enter the following information, and click Save, as shown in Figure 5-19:

1. *Start and End Dates*: These are the dates when the maintenance plan will start and end. All work orders related to the plan must fall within this date range.

2. *Work Type*: Select the work type of work orders you want to generate for the maintenance plan.

3. *Account*: If applicable, select the customer's account.

4. *Work Order Generation Method*: If more than one asset is associated with this maintenance plan, select how you want to generate work orders. Options are one work order for each asset or one work order line item for each asset.

5. *Service Appointment Generation Method*: If the work order generation method is "One work order line item per asset," select the service appointment generation method. Options are one service appointment for the parent work order or one service appointment for each work order line item.

6. *Generation Time Frame and Generation Time Frame Type*: Enter how far in advance you want work orders to be generated. For example, to generate work orders seven days in advance, enter **7** and **days** for the generation time frame and type, respectively.

7. *Date of the first work order in the next batch*: This is the suggested date of service for the first work order, not the date the work order is created. For example, if this date is January 1, the first work order you

generate suggests a maintenance date of January 1, while the dates on later work orders are determined by your selections for the Generation Time Frame and Frequency fields.

8. *Maintenance Window Start (Days) and Maintenance Window End (Days)*: Specify how many days before and after the suggested service date on the work order the service appointments can be scheduled.

9. *Auto-generate work orders*: Select this if you want to generate work orders for the maintenance plan automatically. If this option isn't selected, you must click Generate Work Orders on the maintenance plan to generate a new batch of work orders.

10. *Generate new batch upon completion*: Indicate whether to create the new batch after the final work order in the preceding batch has been completed.

11. *Generation Horizon (Days)*: Specify how many days should pass before the first work order in the following batch is generated. For example, if you specify five days, that means a new batch of work orders is generated five days before the maintenance plan's date of the first work order in the next batch. If you don't specify a generation horizon, it defaults to zero.

12. *Maintenance Plan Title and Description*: Fill in the title and description for the maintenance plan.

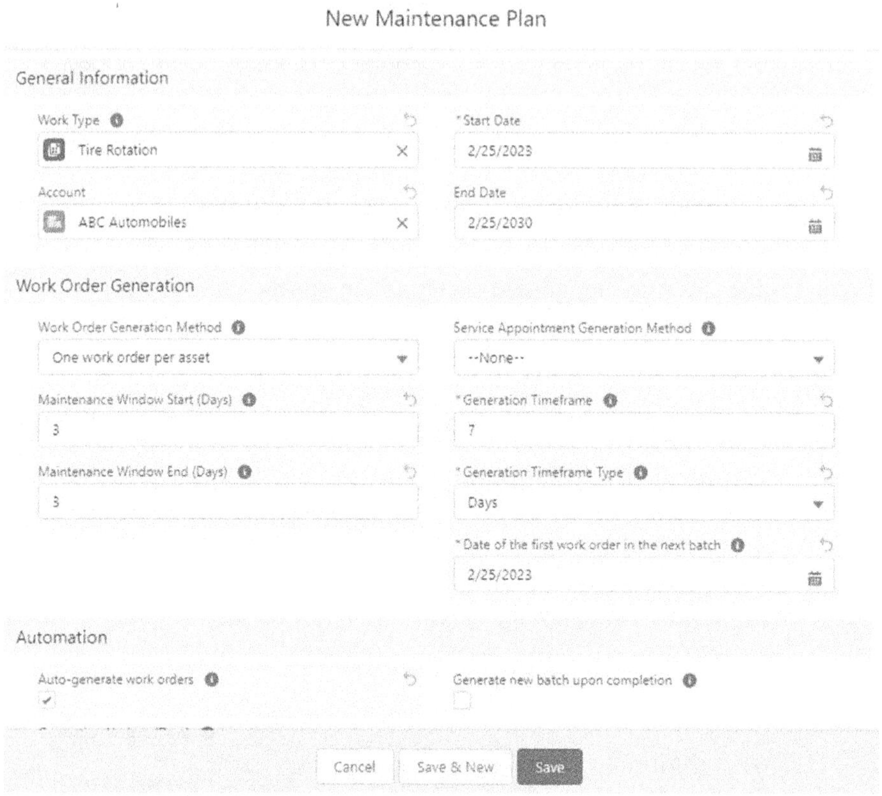

New Maintenance Plan

General Information

Work Type ●   ↺   * Start Date   ↺
  [icon] Tire Rotation   ✕   2/25/2023   📅

Account   ↺   End Date   ↺
  [icon] ABC Automobiles   ✕   2/25/2030   📅

Work Order Generation

Work Order Generation Method ●   Service Appointment Generation Method ●
  One work order per asset   ▼   --None--   ▼

Maintenance Window Start (Days) ●   ↺   * Generation Timeframe ●   ↺
  3   7

Maintenance Window End (Days) ●   ↺   * Generation Timeframe Type ●   ↺
  3   Days   ▼

                                                  * Date of the first work order in the next batch ●   ↺
                                                    2/25/2023   📅

Automation

Auto-generate work orders ●   ↺   Generate new batch upon completion ●
  ✓   ☐

                          Cancel   Save & New   Save

Figure 5-19. *Creating a maintenance plan*

Maintenance plans can be associated with accounts, work types, maintenance assets, locations, and service contracts.

Maintenance Plan Work Rules

Specify conditions and create recurring maintenance plans by using maintenance rules. You can create calendar-based, criteria-based, and usage-based maintenance work rules.

- *Calendar-Based Maintenance Work Rule*: Use this work rule if you want to create monthly or yearly schedules.

- *Criteria-Based Maintenance Work Rule*: Use this work rule if you want to define the criteria that will trigger the service visit. For example, use this maintenance work rule if you want to offer one-time complimentary service to a customer who purchased a car priced over $25,000.

- *Usage-Based Maintenance Work Rule*: Use this work rule if you want to create maintenance schedules based on usage of the asset. For example, if a car is driven for more than 30,000 miles or 3 years, schedule a service visit.

Before setting up maintenance work rules, ensure the following:

- That the Maintenance Work Rules–related list is added to the maintenance plan page layout.

- That the RecordSet Filter Criteria field is added to the Maintenance Work Rule page layout. From the setup, navigate to the Object Manager tab, search for the Maintenance Work Rule object, and navigate to the page layout. If not already added, add RecordSet Filter Criteria field to the page layout.

Calendar-Based Work Rule

To create a calendar based maintenance work rule, follow these steps:

1. Navigate to the maintenance plan you created. Click the Related tab.

2. In the Maintenance Work Rules–related list, click New.

3. Specify the maintenance work title.

4. In the Maintenance Work Rule Type field, select Calendar-based, as shown in Figure 5-20.

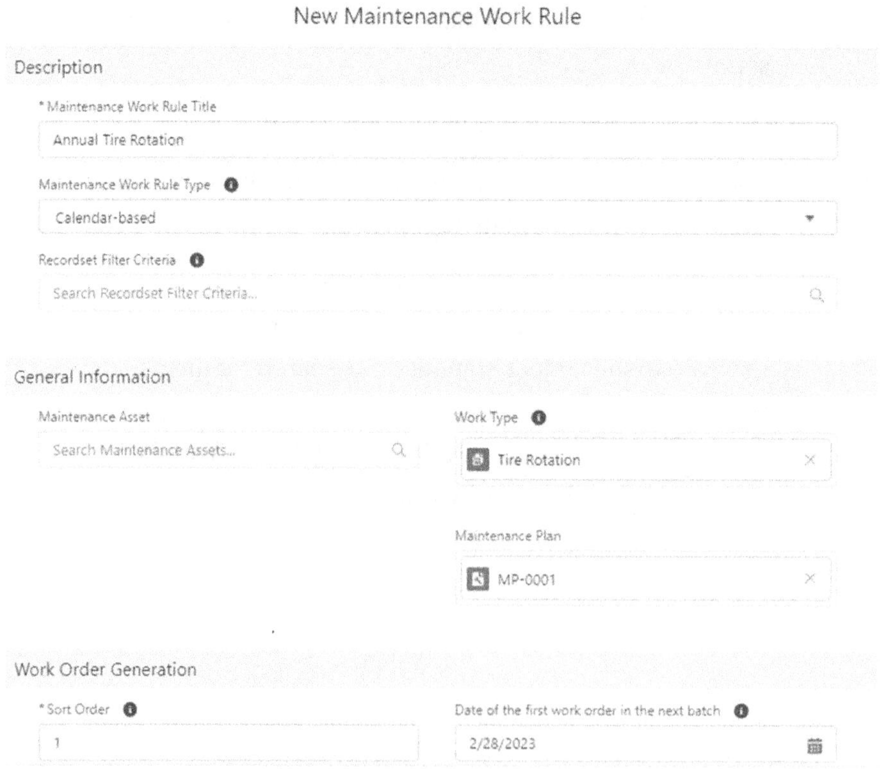

New Maintenance Work Rule

Description

* Maintenance Work Rule Title

Annual Tire Rotation

Maintenance Work Rule Type ⓘ

Calendar-based   ▾

Recordset Filter Criteria ⓘ

Search Recordset Filter Criteria...   🔍

General Information

Maintenance Asset   Work Type ⓘ

Search Maintenance Assets...   🔍   🖼 Tire Rotation   ✕

                                                     Maintenance Plan

                                                     📄 MP-0001   ✕

Work Order Generation

* Sort Order ⓘ   Date of the first work order in the next batch ⓘ

1   2/28/2023   📅

Figure 5-20. *Creating a calendar-based maintenance work rule*

5. Select the work type.

6. If it's not already populated, enter a
    maintenance plan.

7. Specify the sort order. This is the order in which the
    work rules will be executed when multiple work
    rules are added to a maintenance plan. The lowest
    number takes precedence.

8. Specify the date of the first work order in the next
    batch. This date is the suggested date of service
    for the first work order in the next batch. If left
    blank when the maintenance rule is created,
    this field inherits its initial value from the related
    maintenance asset. It auto-updates after each batch
    is generated.

9. In the Reference Pattern section, select the
    recurrence period, frequency, recurring on, and
    recurring end options to indicate how frequently the
    event occurs. See Figure 5-21.

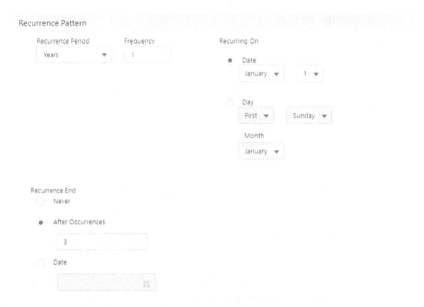

Figure 5-21. *Setting a maintenance rule recurrence pattern*

10. Click Save & New if you want to create more
     maintenance rules; otherwise, click Save.

Criteria-Based Maintenance Work Rule

To create a criteria-based maintenance work rule, first create a RecordSet
filter criteria by following these steps:

1. From the app launcher, search for the Recordset
    Filter Criteria tab.

2. From the Recordset Filter Criteria tab, click New.

3. Enter the recordset filter criteria name and
    description.

4. Under Source Object, select Maintenance Rule.

5. Under Filtered Object, select Asset as asset fields
    will be used to set the criteria.

6. Specify the conditions when the filter criteria
    is valid.

7. Under Rule Type, select Criteria and specify the
    conditions when the maintenance plan is triggered.
    For example, set up a one-time complimentary
    maintenance service to customers if the purchased
    car is more than $25,000, as shown in Figure 5-22,
    and save the recordset filter criteria.

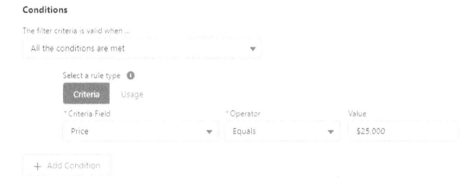

Figure 5-22. *Criteria-based recordset filter criteria*

Usage-Based Maintenance Work Rule

If you want to create a usage-based maintenance rule, repeat the same
steps as for the criteria-based maintenance work rule except under Rule
Type select Usage and specify the conditions when the maintenance plan
is triggered. For example, schedule a maintenance rule every time a car is
driven for more than 30,000 miles, as shown in Figure 5-23.

Conditions

The filter criteria is valid when ...

| All the conditions are met | ▼ |

Select a rule type ⓘ

| Criteria | **Usage** |

*Usage Field		*Next Occurrence Field ⓘ
Miles ▼		Miles ▼

*Frequency ⓘ		*First Occurrence ⓘ	Last Occurrence
30,000		30,000	

| + Add Condition |

Figure 5-23. *Usage-based recordset filter criteria*

Once the recordset filter criteria has been defined, create a new maintenance work rule and include this criteria.

When creating a new maintenance work rule, follow the same steps as when creating a calendar-based maintenance work rule, but instead of choosing Calendar-based, choose Criteria-based and then select the recordset filter criteria, as shown in Figure 5-24.

New Maintenance Work Rule

Description

*Maintenance Work Rule Title

| One time complimentary service |

Maintenance Work Rule Type ⓘ

| Criteria-based | ▼ |

Recordset Filter Criteria ⓘ

| 🔒 Complimentary Service | × |

Figure 5-24. *Creating a criteria-based or usage-based maintenance work rule*

Maintenance Assets

Maintenance assets are used to link assets and the maintenance plan.

To create maintenance assets, ensure you have created both products and assets. Products are goods or services your company offers to the customers, while assets are goods or services purchased or installed by the customer.

To create a product, follow these steps:

1. Navigate to the Products tab from the app launcher.

2. From the Products tab, click New.

3. Enter the product name and other fields as necessary.

4. Select the Active checkbox and click Save. See Figure 5-25.

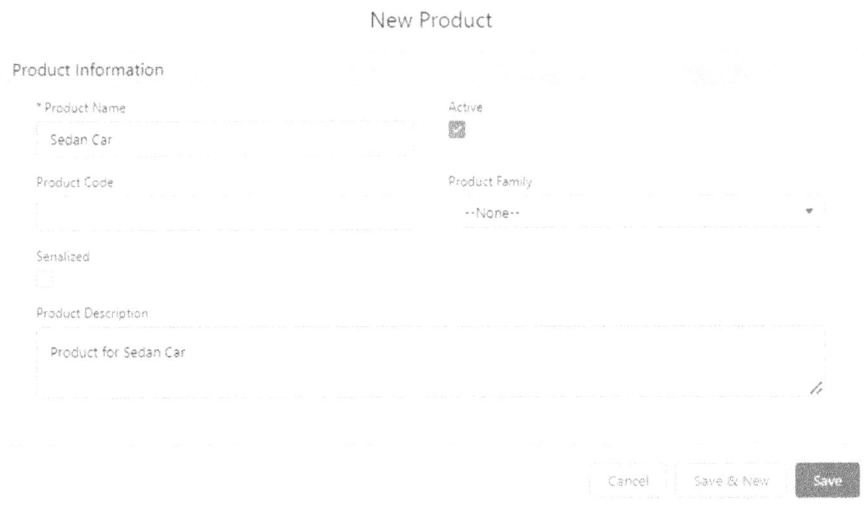

Figure 5-25. *Creating a new product*

To create an asset, follow these steps:

1. Navigate to the Assets tab from the app launcher.

2. From the Assets tab, click New.

3. Enter the asset name.

4. Under the product name, search for the product you just created.

5. Enter the account name and the contact name to represent the customer. Enter a contact that is already associated with the account.

6. Enter the other fields as necessary and click Save. See Figure 5-26.

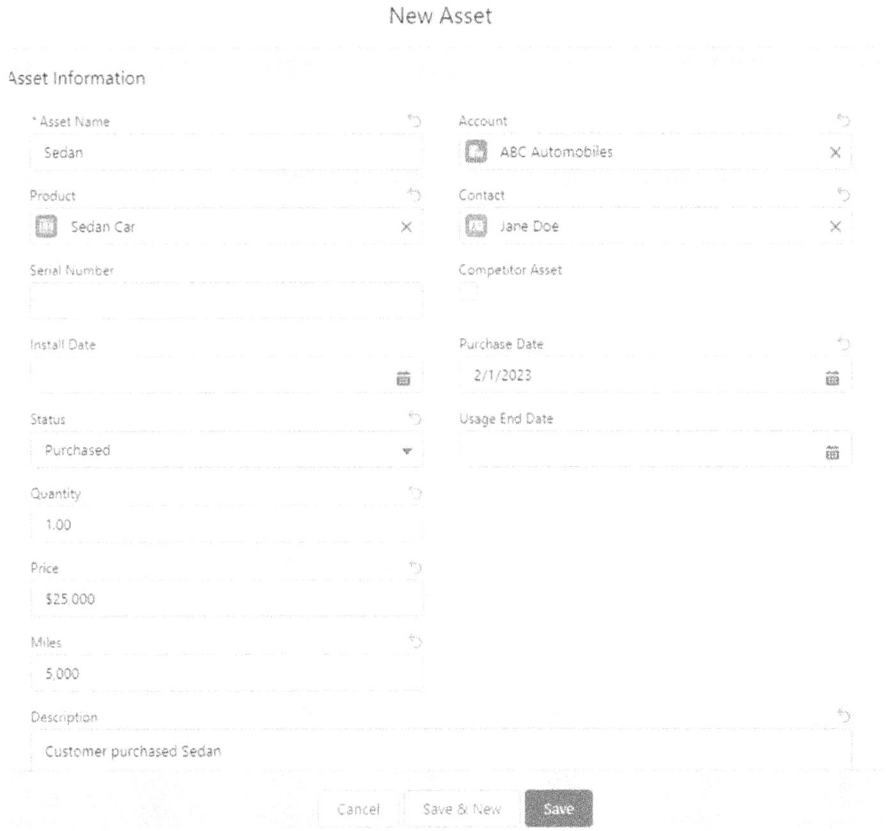

New Asset

Asset Information

* Asset Name

Sedan

Product

Sedan Car

Serial Number

Install Date

Status

Purchased

Quantity

1.00

Price

$25.000

Miles

5.000

Description

Customer purchased Sedan

Account

ABC Automobiles

Contact

Jane Doe

Competitor Asset

Purchase Date

2/1/2023

Usage End Date

Cancel   Save & New   Save

Figure 5-26. *Creating a new asset*

Once the asset is created, create a maintenance asset record to link the asset with the maintenance plan. Ensure the Maintenance Assets–related list is added to the maintenance plan page layout. From the setup, navigate to the Object Manager tab, search for the Maintenance Plan object, and navigate to the page layout. If not already added, add the Maintenance Assets–related list to the page layout.

1. Navigate to the maintenance plan record you created.

2. Click the Related tab.

3. Under the Maintenance Assets–related list, click New.

4. Under Asset, select the asset you just created and click Save.

5. If applicable, enter the work type and date of the first order in the next batch. If you leave these fields blank, they will be autopopulated with the values specified on the maintenance plan. See Figure 5-27.

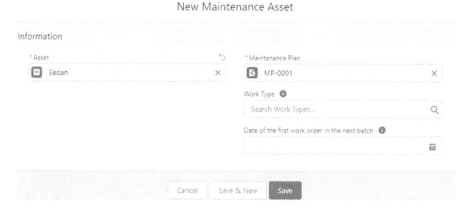

Figure 5-27. *Creating a new maintenance asset*

Generating Work Orders for Maintenance Plans

Let's generate the work orders using the maintenance plan.

Navigate to the maintenance plan record you created. If you have selected the "Auto-generate work orders" checkbox on the maintenance plan, work orders will be automatically generated.

If you want to manually generate the work orders, deselect the "Auto-generate work orders" checkbox, click Save, and then click the Generate Work Orders button in the upper-right corner, as shown in Figure 5-28.

Figure 5-28. *Generating work orders*

Once the work order(s) is successfully generated, the Work Order Generation Status field value changes from Needs Review to Complete.

You can see the generated work orders under the Work Orders–related list of the maintenance plan, as shown in Figure 5-29.

Maintenance Plan Title	Work Type	Start Date	End Date	Date of the first work order in the next batch
Maintenance Plan for Tire Rotation	Tire Rotation	2/25/2023	2/25/2030	2/25/2023

Related   Details

Work Orders (6+)

Work Order Number	Asset	Status	Suggested Maintenance Date	
00000769	Sedan	New	2/27/2023	▼
00000770	Sedan	New	2/28/2023	▼
00000771	Sedan	New	3/1/2023	▼
00000772	Sedan	New	3/2/2023	▼
00000773	Sedan	New	3/3/2023	▼
00000774	Sedan	New	3/4/2023	▼

Figure 5-29. *Work orders associated to the maintenance plan*

Note   The batch size of the work orders generated depends upon the generation timeframe, frequency, and number of assets covered by the plan. A separate work order is created for each maintenance asset for each maintenance date.

The "Generated from maintenance plan" field on the work order will be automatically checked if the work order is generated from a maintenance plan. See Figure 5-30.

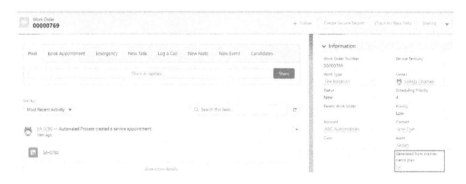

Figure 5-30. *Work order generated from the maintenance plan*

Managing Service Reports

In Field Service, a service report is a summarized PDF document that includes details of the work performed such as description of the work, customer information, asset details, parts used, customer signature, etc.

For generating service reports, first add the service report–related list and the Create Service Report button on the record page layout (work order, work order line item, or service appointment record).

To add the service report–related list and the Create Service Report action to the page layout, follow these steps:

1. On the Object Manager tab in the setup, search for the object you want to add a service report to.

2. Navigate to Page Layouts (on the left side).

3. Under Related Lists, drag and drop the service reports. See Figure 5-31.

Figure 5-31. *Adding a service report–related list to the work order*

4. If it's not already added, add the Create Service Report action to the page layout from the Mobile & Lightning actions.

To create a service report, follow these steps:

1. Navigate to the work order record and click the Create Service Report action. See Figure 5-32.

Figure 5-32. *Creating a service report*

2. Under the service report preview, you should see all
    the information related to the work order, customer,
    address, and parts.

    - When clicking Create and Send Service Report, an
      email action will pop up with an attached service
      report to send to the customer or team members.

    - If you don't want to send the service report, click
      Create Service Report. This action will generate the
      service report and add it to the Service Reports–
      related list on the Related tab of the record. See
      Figure 5-33.

Figure 5-33. *Service report preview*

The service report will be saved under the service reports–related list of the work order, as shown in Figure 5-34.

Figure 5-34. *Service reports–related list*

Service Report Template

You can create service report templates to get more control over what appears in your service reports. You can create standard or custom service report templates for work orders, work order line items, or service appointments.

To create a service report template, follow these steps:

1. From the setup, in the Quick Find box, enter **Service report** and select Service Report Templates.

2. Click Edit next to the standard template to edit the existing standard template.

3. Click New to create a custom service report template.

4. Select an existing template to build on and enter the template name.

5. Under Related Templates, select a subtemplate. The subtemplate indicates the record type for which the layout is being edited.

6. Drag and drop the fields you want to see on the service report template.

7. Click Quick Save. See Figure 5-35.

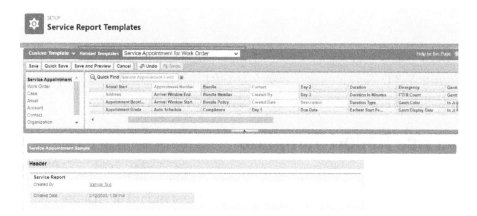

Figure 5-35. *Service report template layout*

Each template comes with four subtemplates, which enables service reports for multiple record types.

•   Service Appointment for Work Order

•   Service Appointment for Work Order Line Item

•   Work Order

•   Work Order Line Item

Customize all four subtemplates so that your service reports contain the right information.

8. Repeat steps (5) to (7) for editing other subtemplates.

9. Click Save and Preview to preview the service report template.

10. Click Activate next to the template name on the Service Report Templates home page.

You can update the Service Report Template field on the work type, as shown in Figure 5-36, to choose a service report template for the work type so that every time a work order or work order line item is created with the work type, the related service report template is selected.

Figure 5-36. Service report template for work type

Note   Work orders or work order line items that don't include a service report template use the associated work type's service report template. If the work type doesn't provide a template or if no work type is given, the work order or work order line item utilizes the default service report template.

Using the Dispatcher Console

The dispatcher console serves as the dispatcher's primary workspace. It has a dynamic map and a Gantt chart that can be used to manage upcoming appointments, schedules, and service resources. In this section, you will understand how to use and customize the dispatcher console in detail. To access the dispatcher console, ensure you have given yourself the right permissions and licenses, as specified in Chapter 3.

The dispatcher console can be reached from the app launcher. Go to the Field Service app and then the Field Service tab, as shown in Figure 5-37. The system will check for all the permissions and open the dispatcher console.

Figure 5-37. *Accessing the dispatcher console*

Once you launch the dispatcher console, you can see all the service appointments on the left side and the Gantt chart/map on the right side, as shown in Figure 5-38.

Figure 5-38. *Dispatcher console view*

In this section, we will be using the dispatcher console to do the following:

- View, schedule, and dispatch the service appointments to the right candidates

- Explore the Gantt chart

- Explore the map

View, schedule, and dispatch service appointments using the dispatcher console.

Let's take a look at the service appointments on the left side. Figure 5-39 indicates all the elements used to retrieve and manage service appointments.

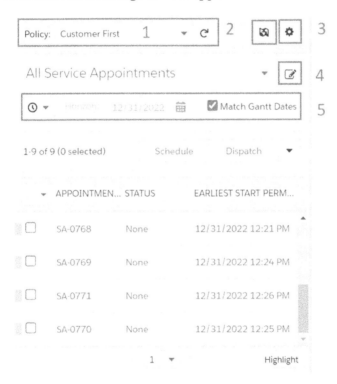

Figure 5-39. *Dispatcher console service appointments list*

Policy (1): To select the scheduling policy used for scheduling appointments.

Territories icon (2): To filter service appointments that are not associated to the service territories.

Settings icon (3): To change the look of the appointment list.

Filter icon (4): To edit the filter to display the service appointments.

Horizon (5): The service appointments within the horizon date will be displayed in the dispatcher console. This will work when Match Gantt Dates is not selected. The horizon date updates to reflect the dates displayed on the Gantt chart if you choose Match Gantt Dates.

To assign service appointments to the right candidates, do one of the following:

- Drag and drop the service appointment onto the Gantt chart against the preferred service resource slot.

- Select the service appointment, and click Candidates to look for available service resources. See Figure 5-40.

Figure 5-40. *Dispatcher console's Candidates action*

You should see all the qualified candidates for scheduling, as shown in Figure 5-41. You can group slots either by service resources or by dates available. Based on the resource availability, the scheduler grades and recommends the best candidates for scheduling.

Showing candidates to SA-0768   Hide Slots

We found **4** candidates with a total of **20** slots for **SA-0768**. The recommended scheduling is for **Jane Doe** on **Sun, Jan 1, 2023 8:22 AM** (Graded **91**/100).

ASSIGN RECOMMENDED

Group slots by: ◉ Service Res...   ○   Date   ⓘ

	Andrew Smith 5 options	91/100
	Jacky Gill 5 options	91/100
	Jane Doe 5 options	91/100
	John Smith 5 options	91/100

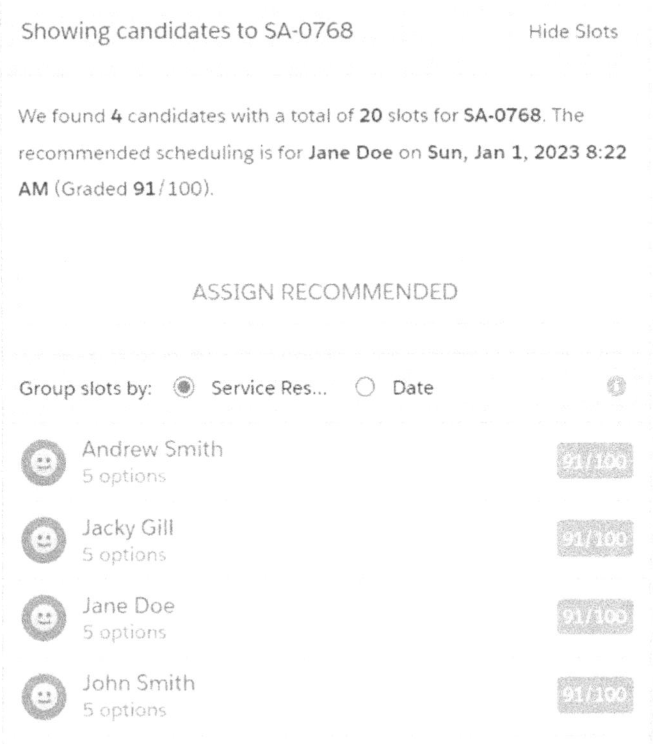

Figure 5-41. *Dispatcher console recommended candidates*

Click the candidate's name to see their time slots. To schedule an appointment, click Schedule next to the time slot. See Figure 5-42.

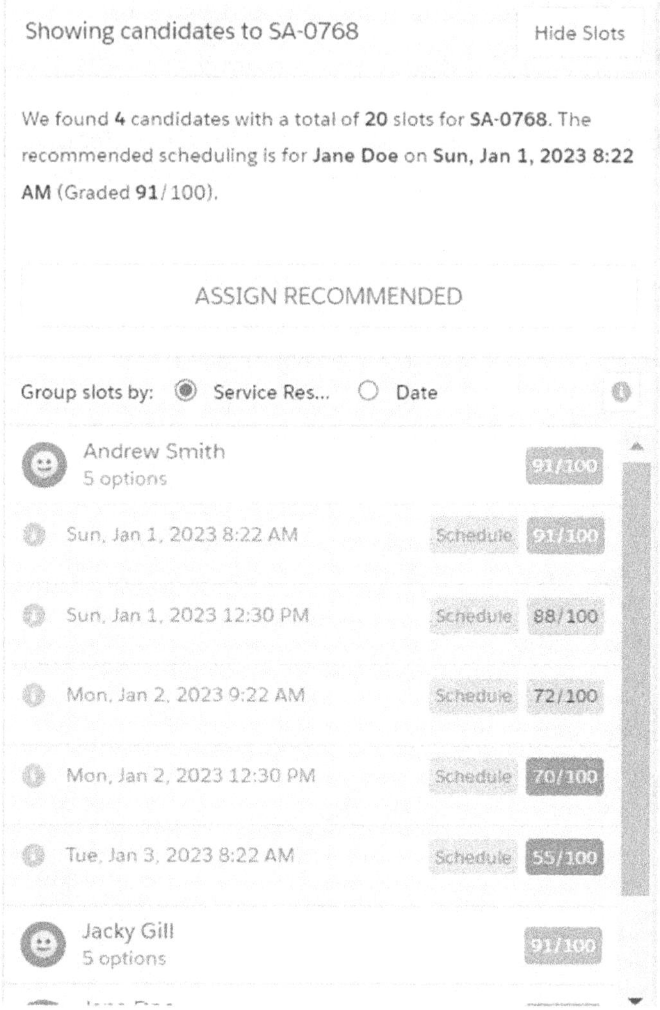

Figure 5-42. *Dispatcher console's Schedule action*

Once the service appointment is scheduled, the next step is to dispatch the appointment.

To dispatch an appointment, follow these steps:

1. Navigate back to the service appointments list on the left side of the dispatcher console.

2. Right-click the scheduled appointment, expand the drop-down for actions, and select Dispatch, as shown in Figure 5-43.

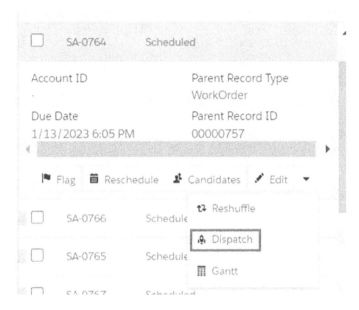

Figure 5-43. *Dispatcher console's Dispatch action*

Once dispatched, the status of the appointment changes to dispatched from scheduled. A notification is sent to the mobile worker's phone when an appointment is dispatched.

To perform bulk actions on the service appointments, select the service appointments and click Schedule or Dispatch for bulk scheduling or dispatching. Click the drop-down to explore more bulk actions, as shown in Figure 5-44.

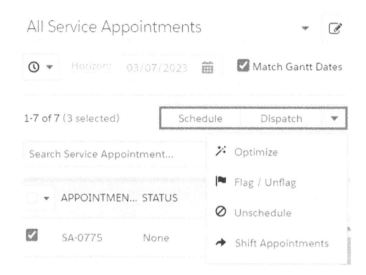

Figure 5-44. *Bulk actions on service appointments*

Gantt

The Gantt chart on the right side displays the schedules for service resources based on the selected service territories. See Figure 5-45.

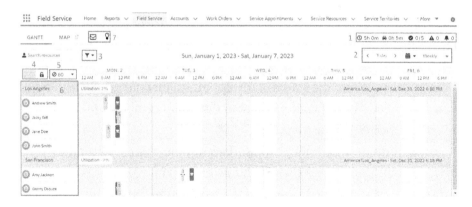

Figure 5-45. *Dispatcher console's Gantt chart*

Key performance indicator bar (1): The indicators, from left to right, are as follows:

- Total scheduled time (workload) of all loaded service territories

- Average travel time per service appointment of all service appointments shown on the Gantt chart

- Number of completed service appointments out of all service appointments shown on the Gantt chart

- Number of service appointments on the Gantt chart with rule violations

- Number of service appointments on the Gantt chart that are in jeopardy

Calendar and Gantt Resolution drop-down list (2): Use the calendar to show appointments for specific dates. Use the arrows to toggle between days and months. Click the Gantt Resolution drop-down to select how many days to show on the Gantt chart at once. You can choose Days, Weeks, or Long Term. Select Utilization to show the resource utilization. See Figure 5-46.

Figure 5-46. *Viewing the resource utilization*

Filter icon (3): To filter service resources that appear on the Gantt chart, you can filter by the following:

- *Hours*: Select the hours window to show on the Gantt chart. The Gantt time interval and how available hours are displayed depend on the date resolution.

- *Resources*: Specify which service resources are shown and in what order.

- *Skills*: Select skills that resources must possess to be shown on the Gantt chart.

- *Utilization*: Select the factors that are considered when calculating resource utilization, and control the days shown in the utilization view.

- *Palettes*: Create, manage, and apply palettes to color-code service appointments on the Gantt chart and map.

Gantt Locker (4): Lock and unlock the Gantt chart using the Gantt locker. This action disables dragging appointments to the Gantt chart from the appointment list or map. Without this permission, Gantt access is read-only.

Set Non Availability (5): Set the nonavailability duration and click the drop-down to specify the absence reason and label. Drag and drop it onto the Gantt chart to display it. See Figure 5-47.

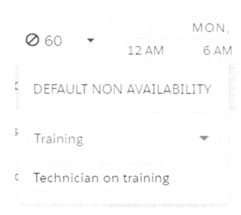

Figure 5-47. *Setting nonavailability*

Service Resources (6): List of service resources grouped by territories. Click the resource name to see more details.

Notifications and optimizations requests (7): Click the email and bulb icon in the dispatcher console header to see the notifications and optimization requests.

Rule Violations on the Gantt

Sometimes you can see the rule violation ⚠ icon on the service appointment. These violations typically occur as a result of manual scheduling when the service appointments are scheduled outside of the scheduling rules. Some examples of rule violations could be that service appointments are scheduled outside of operating hours set by resource, travel time conflicts, or appointments that aren't scheduled between their earliest start permitted and due date.

Hover over the service appointment to see more details about the violation. See Figure 5-48.

Figure 5-48. *Rule violation details*

The scheduling policy selected at the top of the appointment list controls which rules are applied.

When service appointments are automatically scheduled using Schedule or Candidates actions, these rule violations don't occur as Field Service automatically formulates schedules that don't violate rules.

Map

Dispatchers can see a bird's-eye view of their mobile workforce on the dispatcher console map. By default, the map shows markers for all service resources whose appointments are loaded in the Gantt chart or appointment list. Click the Map tab to access the map. See Figure 5-49.

Figure 5-49. *Dispatcher console's map*

To control what appears on the map, click Map Layers. See Figure 5-50.

Figure 5-50. *Map layers*

On the Markers tab, choose which objects you want to see on the map.

- *Live Positions*: The coordinates of a service resource are automatically saved when they update the status of a service appointment from a mobile device. The most recent system-saved coordinates are displayed in Live Position.

- *Homebase*: This is the selected service resource's address as specified on their service resource record.

- *Service Appointments*: These are all service appointments that are displayed in the appointment list and assigned to the chosen service resource.

- *Service Territories*: These are the resource's service territories.

On the Service Resources tab, select the resources to be displayed on the map.

On Report Data, select the reports containing geolocation fields that you want to be displayed on the map.

On the Polygons tab, create a new polygon to draw your own field service territory directly on the map. With Polygons, you can bulk update all appointments within a specific geographic area.

You can customize Gantt charts, add custom actions, and add reports to display on the map from the dispatcher console UI in the Field Service Settings.

Summary

Overall, managing Salesforce Field Service capabilities involves ensuring that your organization is effectively using Salesforce's tools and features to manage field service operations. Here are some key pointers to remember:

- Service resources can use timesheets to track their time and work using mobile devices. Timesheets are composed of timesheet entries. Timesheet entries typically track individual tasks. Use timesheet templates to automatically create time sheets for your service resources.

- Create a service crew and add service resources to the crew to represent a team that will be completing a task as a unit. You can use the Service Crews tab in the app launcher or Crew Management Tool to create service crews.

- Indicate a resource's unavailability using resource absences. This allows the scheduler to not assign appointments when the resources are unavailable.

- Set up preventive maintenance plans for assets so that work orders are generated automatically and customers do not lose out on anything. Create maintenance rules to specify criteria for the maintenance plan. Use the maintenance asset to link the maintenance plan with an asset.

- Use a service report to summarize the details of the work performed and get customer signatures. If you want to control which fields are visible on the service report, use service report templates.

- The dispatcher console is used as a central workplace for dispatchers to view, filter, and schedule all the service appointments. Dispatchers can track all the service resources, service appointments, and service territories using the Gantt and map tools.

The following chapter will cover inventory management, which is yet another key component of Salesforce Field Service.

CHAPTER 6

Inventory Management

Effective inventory management helps ensure that the necessary equipment and materials are available for field service technicians when they need them. This reduces downtime and enables technicians to complete jobs faster, resulting in increased productivity and customer satisfaction.

By maintaining accurate inventory records, businesses can better control their costs by minimizing overstocking or understocking of inventory. This ensures that they order only what they need, reducing waste and increasing profitability.

In this chapter, you will learn about several objects involved in Salesforce inventory management, their data models, and how to set them up to maintain an up-to-date inventory.

Inventory Management Use Case

Let's return to the ABC Automobiles use case, discussed in Chapter 3. Technicians should be able to check which vehicle parts are needed to complete a work order and which inventory locations have the parts available. When the stock runs out, they should be able to request more parts from another inventory location. Parts may be transferred between inventory locations or from a vendor to an inventory location as needed. Additionally, if parts are damaged or unused, technicians should be able to request a return.

Inventory Management Objects and Data Model

Before setting up the inventory, let's first comprehend the numerous objects that go into managing it. All the inventory management objects can be grouped into the categories shown in Figure 6-1.

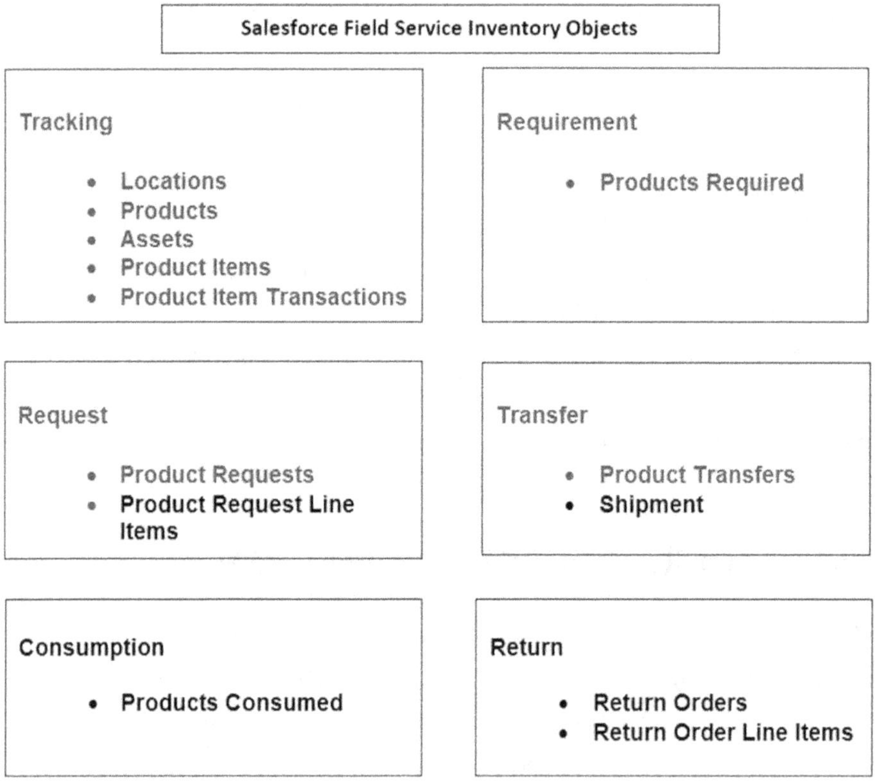

Figure 6-1. *Salesforce Field Service inventory objects*

Locations are places where inventory is stored. Examples of locations could be warehouses, sites, work vehicles, factories, etc. Create locations so you can track the items stored there and restock when necessary.

Products represent parts needed to complete a job.

Product items are products in your inventory stored at a particular location. For example, if you have 20 tires stored in location A and 10 tires stored in location B, create one product item for each location. Create product items so you can track inventory usage and restock when necessary. Product items list a quantity at the location that is updated automatically when inventory is transferred or consumed.

Product item transactions are actions performed on a product item. They're autogenerated records that help you track when a product item is replenished, consumed, or adjusted.

Products required are products that are needed to complete a work order or work order line item.

Products consumed are product items that were used to complete a work order or work order line item and are no longer in your inventory.

Product requests are orders for products, which you might create when stock is running low. **Product request line items** are subdivisions of a product request. Create a single product request line item to track each part.

Product transfers track the transfer of product items between inventory locations.

Return orders track the return or repair of products.

Return order line items are subdivisions of a return order. Create a single return order line item to track each part.

Shipments represent the shipment of product items between locations.

Assets are products purchased by the customers.

Figure 6-2 demonstrates how these objects are interlinked with each other.

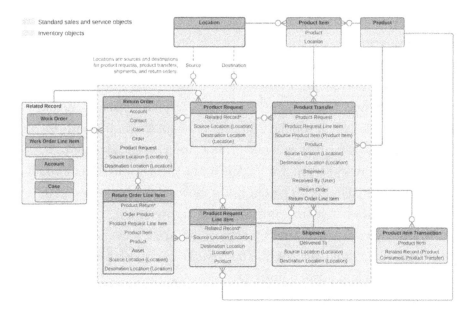

Figure 6-2. *Field Service inventory management data model(Source: developer.salesforce.com)*

Configuring Inventory

The following sections detail how you configure an inventory.

Setting Up Inventory Locations

Let's start by creating inventory locations in Salesforce.

1. First, ensure all the necessary fields and related lists are added to the location page layout. From the setup, navigate to the Object Manager tab, search for the Location object, and navigate to the page layout, as shown in Figure 6-3.

If they're not already added, add the following fields
to the page layout:

- *Inventory Location* to track where inventory
  is stored

- *Mobile Location* to flag mobile locations such as
  service vehicles

- *Parent Location* to create location hierarchies

If they're not already added, add the following
related lists to the page layout:

- *Addresses* to show addresses related to the location,
  such as billing and shipping addresses.

- *Associated Locations* to show related accounts.

- *Child Locations* to show locations within the
  location, such as vehicles that are parked at a
  warehouse when not in use.

- *Maintenance Plans* to show maintenance plans
  linked to the location.

- *Product Items* to show product items (inventory)
  stored at the location.

- *Product Transfers (Source)* to show product
  transfers that originated at the location.

- *Product Transfers (Destination)* to show product
  transfers in which items were transferred to the
  location.

- *Service Territory Locations* to show related service
  territories, which usually indicates that the location
  is within the territory.

- *Assets* to show assets at the location. Assets represent products purchased or installed by customers. See Figure 6-3.

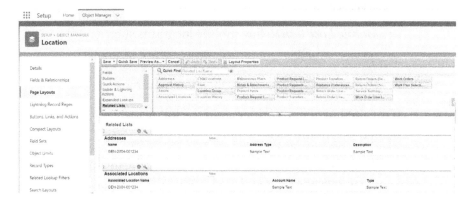

Figure 6-3. *Location page layout*

2. To create a location, from the app launcher, search for the Locations tab.

    a. From the Locations tab, click New.

    b. Enter the location name and type. Optionally, you can customize the values in the Location Type field. Its default values are Warehouse, Van, Site, and Plant.

    c. Select the Inventory Location checkbox if the inventory is stored at the location. Do not skip this step because this will allow you to associate locations with product items in your inventory.

    d. Select the Mobile Location checkbox if the location is movable like van or toolbox.

    e. Enter all other fields as needed and click Save. See Figure 6-4.

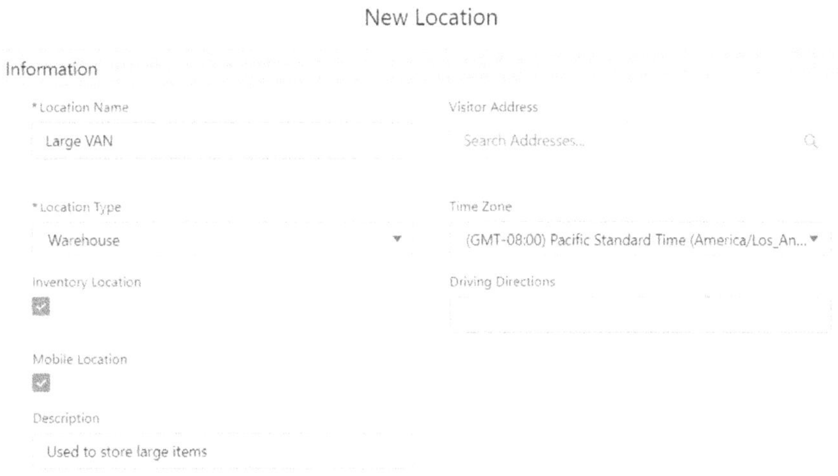

New Location

Information

* Location Name

Large VAN

* Location Type

Warehouse ▼

Inventory Location
☑

Mobile Location
☑

Description

Used to store large items

Visitor Address

Search Addresses... 🔍

Time Zone

(GMT-08:00) Pacific Standard Time (America/Los_An... ▼

Driving Directions

Figure 6-4. *Creation new inventory location*

f. As shown in Figure 6-5, navigate to the Related tab. Under the Addresses related list, click New to create addresses for the location. The available types of addresses are Mailing, Shipping, Billing, and Home. Under the Service Territory Locations–related list, create records to indicate which service territories the location belongs to. Service territory locations are warehouses, customer sites, or vehicles that are located or operate in the service territory.

If needed, you can update other related lists for the location. For example, you can add files related to the location, create product items, create child locations, create maintenance plans for the location, etc. See Figure 6-5.

Figure 6-5. *Updating related lists for the location*

Setting Up Product Items

Product items represent your inventory. Each product item is linked to a storage location (van or warehouse) and to a specific product, indicating the item being stored.

To set up product items, follow these steps:

1. First, ensure all the necessary fields and related lists are added to the product item page layout. From the setup, navigate to the Object Manager tab, search for the Product Item object, and navigate to the page layout, as shown in Figure 6-6.

    If they're not already added, add the following fields to the page layout:

    • *Location* to track where product items are stored.

    • *Quantity On Hand* to track the quantity of the product item at the location. Product item quantities auto-update to reflect transfers between locations.

160

- *Quantity Unit Of Measure* to specify units of the product item, for example, kilograms or liters. Quantity Unit of Measure picklist values are inherited from the Quantity Unit of Measure field on products.

- Optionally, *Serial Number* to specify a unique number for product item identification. If you assign a serial number, each product item represents a single item in your inventory. For example, create one product item representing a tire with serial number 20230218 stored at location XYZ.

If they're not already added, add the following related lists to the page layout:

- *Product Item Transactions* related list to automatically track the replenishment, consumption, and adjustment of product items

- *Product Transfers* related list to show transfers of the inventory

Figure 6-6. *Product item page layout*

2. Create products to associate with the product item. To create a product, from the app launcher, search for the Products tab.

    a. From the Products tab, click New.

    b. Enter the product name and other fields as necessary.

    c. Select the Active checkbox and click Save. See Figure 6-7.

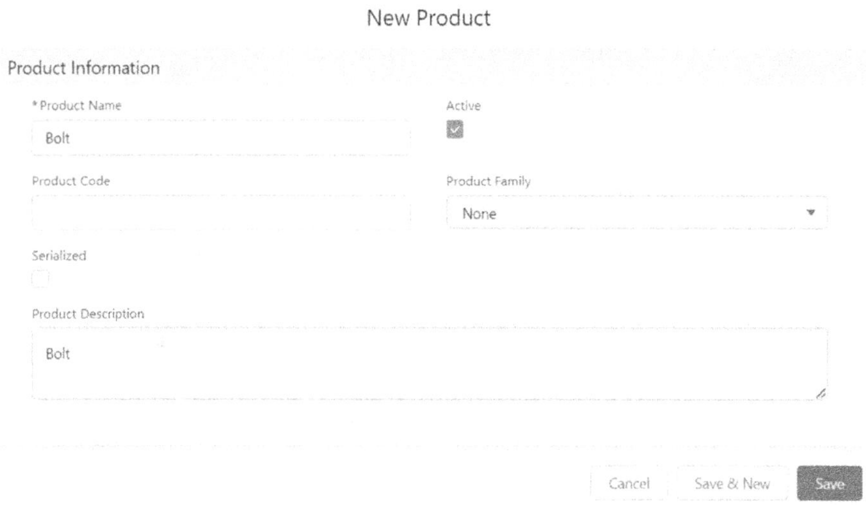

New Product

Product Information

*Product Name

Bolt

Active

Product Code

Product Family

None

Serialized

Product Description

Bolt

Cancel   Save & New   Save

Figure 6-7. *Creating a new product*

3. To create a product item, from the app launcher,
   search for the Product Items tab.

   a. From the Product Items tab, click New.

   b. Under the Product Name lookup field, search and
      select the product you created.

   c. Under the Location lookup field, search and
      select the location where you want to store the
      product item.

   d. Enter something for the Quantity on Hand and
      Quantity Unit of Measure fields.

   e. Click Save. See Figure 6-8.

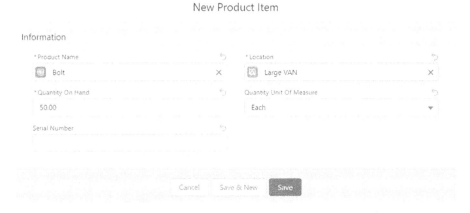

Figure 6-8. *Creating a new product item*

As shown in Figure 6-9, under the Product Item Transaction related
list, you will notice the following:

- When creating a product item, a new product item
  transaction is created with the Replenished type that
  tells you when the product item was created.

- When updating the product item, a new product item transaction is created with the Adjusted type and a quantity that is the difference between the old and new Quantity On Hand value.

- When deleting a product item, all product item transactions are deleted. See Figure 6-9.

Product Item Transactions (2)			
Product Item Transaction Number	Related Record	Transaction Type	Quantity
T-005		Adjusted	-1.00
T-004		Replenished	50.00
		View All	

Figure 6-9. *Product item transactions*

The product item will also appear under the Product Items related list of the associated product and location records.

Setting Up Required Products

You can add products required to work types, work orders, and work order line items to ensure your workforce has the right equipment for the job.

Since work orders and work order line items inherit products required from their work type, adding the required products to work types saves time and regularizes your service process. For instance, a car jack or lug wrench is needed to perform tire rotation. These two items can be added as required for the Tire Rotation work type.

To add products required for work type, follow these steps:

1. Ensure the Products Required–related list is added to the work type page layout. From the setup, navigate to the Object Manager tab, search for the Work Type object, and navigate to the page layout. If it's not already added, add the Products Required–related list to the page layout.

2. To add the products required, from the app launcher, search for the Work Types tab.

   a. From the Work Types tab, click the work type record for adding required products.

   b. Click the Related tab.

   c. Under the Products Required–related list, click New.

   d. Under the Product Required lookup, search for the product.

   e. Enter values for Quantity Required and Quantity Unit Of Measure.

   f. Click Save. See Figure 6-10.

Figure 6-10. *Assigning required products*

Repeat steps 1 and 2 to add the required products to the work order or work order line item records.

Requesting Products

In routine field service situations, you might require a specific part to finish a work order or you might need to replenish your inventory. You can submit a product request in such circumstances. Each product request can be divided into line items where each line item represents a needed part. You can request a product for work order, work order line item, case, or account.

To create a product request, follow these steps:

1. Ensure the Product Requests–related list is added to the work order page layout. From the setup, navigate to the Object Manager tab, search for the Work Order object, and navigate to the page layout. If not already added, add the Product Requests–related list to the page layout.

2. To add a product request, from the app launcher, search for the Work Orders tab.

   a. From the Work Orders tab, click the work order record for which parts are needed.

   b. Click the Related tab.

   c. Under the Product Requests–related list, click New.

   d. Under the Destination Location lookup field, search for the location where the parts are needed.

   e. Under the Ship to Address field, enter the address where the parts should be shipped, for example, the shipping address of the warehouse that is requesting them.

   f. Keep the status as Draft.

g. Under the Shipment Type field, select a shipment speed.

h. Under the Need By Date field, specify the date by which parts should be delivered.

i. Click Save. See Figure 6-11.

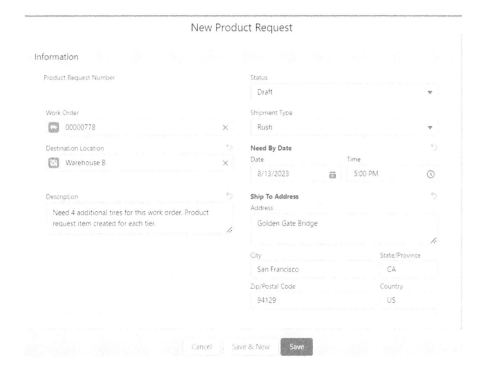

Figure 6-11. *Requesting products*

3. Create one product request line item for each product needed, as shown in Figure 6-12.

a. Under the Product Request record, click the Related tab.

b. Under the Product Request Line Items–related list, click New.

Figure 6-12. *Product request line item related list*

    c. As shown in Figure 6-13, fill in the necessary
       information. The parent product request's shipping
       and related record information is autopopulated on
       its line items.

    d. Click Save & New to request more parts; otherwise,
       click Save. See Figure 6-13.

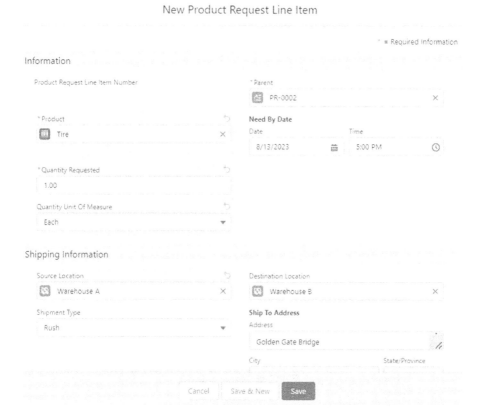

Figure 6-13. *Creating a new product request line item*

Repeat steps 1, 2, and 3 to create product requests for work order line items, accounts, or case records.

Transfer Inventory

Product transfers are generally made in response to a product request. You can track the transfers for each part by creating a product transfer record for each product request line item. The Product Transfers–related list on a product request shows all product transfers associated with the request's line items. The quantity of the inventory is auto-updated to reflect the transfer.

You can create product transfers on the following object records:

- Product Request

- Product Request Line Item

- Product Item

- Location

- Shipment

To create a product transfer for a product request record, follow these steps:

1. Ensure the Product Transfers–related list is added to the product request page layout. From the setup, navigate to the Object Manager tab, search for the Product Request object, and navigate to the page layout. If not already added, add the Product Transfers–related list to the page layout. Similarly, navigate to the Product Request Line Item object and add the Product Transfers–related list to the product request line item page layout.

2. Confirm the product transfer has all the relevant fields. From the setup, navigate to the Object Manager tab, search for the Product Transfers object, and navigate to the page layout. If they're not already added, add the following fields to the product transfer page layout:

   - *Product Name*: The product associated with the product transfer.

   - *Source Product Item*: The product item representing the stock at the source location.

- *Quantity Sent*: The amount of product sent from the source location.

- *Quantity Received*: The amount of product received at the destination location.

- *Quantity Unit of Measure*: The units of the product, e.g., kilograms or liters. The picklist values are inherited from the related product.

- *Product Request Line Item*: The product request line item associated with the product transfer.

- *Shipment*: The shipment related to the product transfer.

- *Source Location*: The location where the product is coming from.

- *Destination Location*: The location where the product is to be delivered.

- *Expected Pickup Date*: The date the product is expected to be picked up.

- *Received*: Indicates that the product was received. See Figure 6-14.

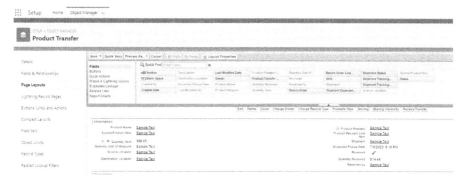

Figure 6-14. *Product transfer page layout*

3. Optionally, link shipments to product transfers so that your team is always aware of the status of transfers and exchange of items in your inventory.

    a. From the app launcher, search for the Shipments tab. From the Shipments tab, click New.

    b. In the General Information section, add details about the shipment's origin and destination. If applicable, select the field service locations where the shipment departs or arrives.

    c. In the Tracking Information section, add details about the shipping provider and delivery date.

    d. Add a description and click Save. See Figure 6-15.

New Shipment

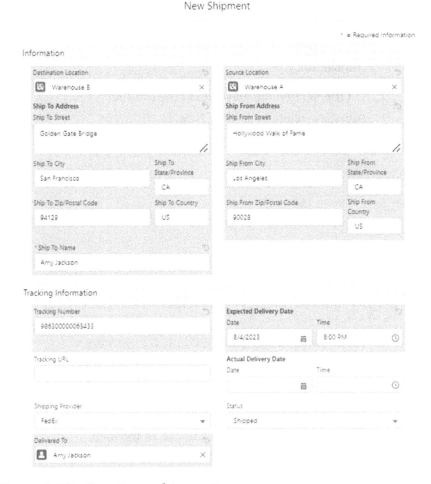

Figure 6-15. *Creating a shipment*

4. To add a product transfer from the product request
    record, search for the Product Requests tab from the
    app launcher.

    a. From the Product Requests tab, click a product
        request record.

b. On the Related tab, navigate to the product
request line items–related list and click a product
request line item record that you want to track the
transfer for.

c. On the Related tab, navigate to the product
transfers–related list, click New, as shown in
Figure 6-16.

Figure 6-16. *Product Transfers–related list*

d. Fill in the product name field only for transfers
outside the inventory, such as receiving products
from a manufacturer.

e. Fill in the source product item field for transfers
within the inventory. For example, to transfer
25 bolts from location A to location B, select the
product item record that tracks the bolts stored at
location A.

f. Under the Quantity Sent and Quantity Unit of
Measure fields, enter the quantity to transfer and the
unit of measurement.

g. If it's not already populated, enter the related product request
line item.

h. Under the Shipment lookup field, select the shipment you created.

i. Enter the source and destination location.

j. Enter the expected pickup date.

k. Click Save. See Figure 6-17.

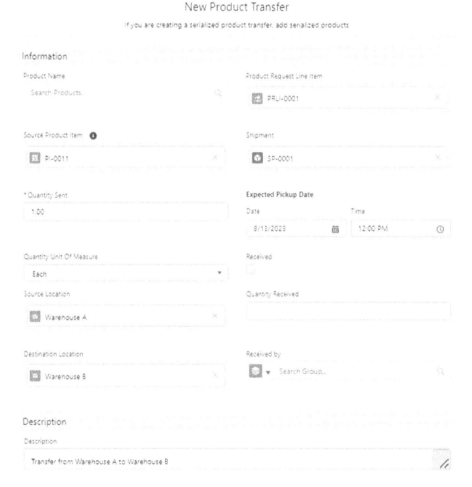

Figure 6-17. *Creating a product transfer*

After the transferred parts are received, select the Received field and update the following:

- Received By

- Quantity Received

- Status

After you mark a product transfer as received, you can't undo it. You will see the product item transactions are automatically tracked under the Product Item Transactions–related list, as shown in Figure 6-18.

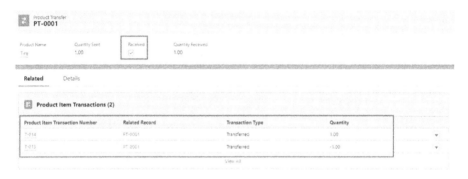

Figure 6-18. *Product item transactions for product item transferred*

Tracking Inventory Consumption

You can track products consumed to complete a job so that your inventory numbers are adjusted accordingly. Products consumed can be added to work orders or work order line items. Track product consumption at the line item level if you want to know which products were used for each line item's tasks.

To create a consumed product, follow these steps:

1. Ensure the Product Consumed–related list is added to the work order or work order line item page layout. From the setup, navigate to the Object Manager tab, search for the Work Order or Work Order Line Item object, and navigate to the page layout. If not already added, add the Products Consumed–related list to the page layout.

2. To add a product consumed, from the app launcher, search for the Work Orders tab.

   a. From the Work Orders tab, click the work order record.

   b. On the Related tab, navigate to the Products Consumed–related list, and click New.

   c. Under Product Item, select the item that was consumed from the location. For example, select the tire stored in location A if it was used to complete the work order.

   d. Under Quantity Consumed, enter the number of parts consumed.

   e. If applicable, fill in the price book entry and unit price.

   f. If applicable, fill in the related work order line item.

   g. Add a description and click Save. See Figure 6-19.

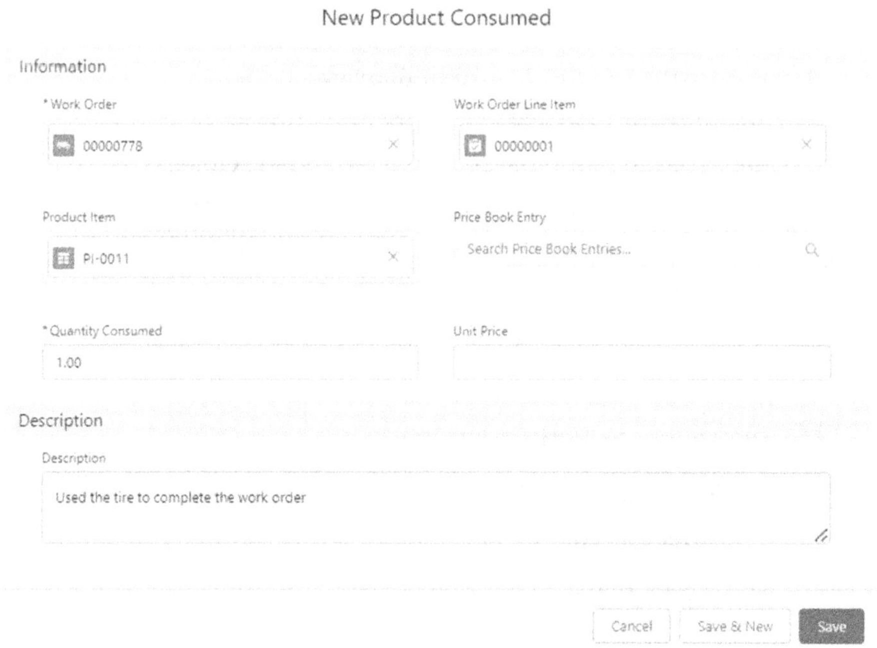

New Product Consumed

Information

* Work Order

🗒 00000778   ×

Work Order Line Item

📄 00000001   ×

Product Item

🔳 PI-0011   ×

Price Book Entry

Search Price Book Entries...   🔍

* Quantity Consumed

1.00

Unit Price

Description

Description

Used the tire to complete the work order

Cancel   Save & New   **Save**

Figure 6-19. *Creating a Product Consumed record*

Once you save the Product Consumed record, go to the Related
tab and see how the consumed transaction for the product item is
automatically shown with quantity and transaction type under the Product
Item Transactions–related list. See Figure 6-20.

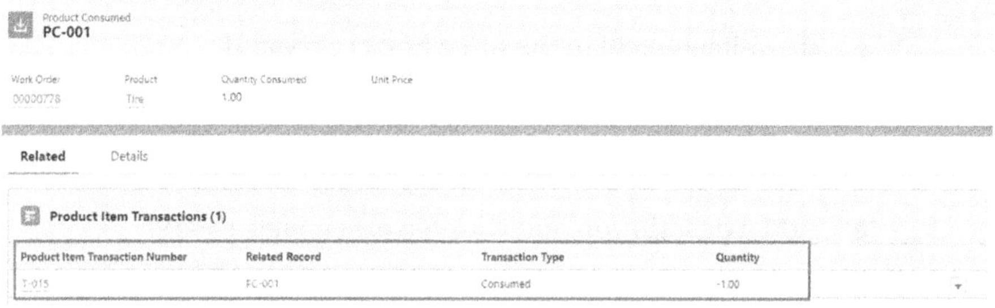

Product Consumed
PC-001

| Work Order | Product | Quantity Consumed | Unit Price |
| 00000778 | Tire | 1.00 | |

Related   Details

🔳 **Product Item Transactions (1)**

Product Item Transaction Number	Related Record	Transaction Type	Quantity	
T-015	PC-001	Consumed	-1.00	▾

Figure 6-20. *Product item transaction for product item consumed*

Tracking Return Orders

You can create return orders to track returned items from a customer or a field service personnel. This is needed when a customer or technician returns a defective product, cancels an order, or returns excess inventory. Return Order Line Item represents a particular item that is sent back or fixed as part of a return order in Field Service. Return orders are normally created from the product requests records.

1. Ensure the Return Orders–related list is added to the product request page layout. From the setup, navigate to the Object Manager tab, search for the Product Request or Product Request Line Item object, and navigate to the page layout. If it's not already added, add the Return Orders–related list to the page layout.

2. To create a return order from the product request record, search for the Product Requests tab from the app launcher.

   a. Click the product request record for which you want to create a return order.

   b. On the Related tab, navigate to the Return Orders related list and click New, as shown in Figure 6-21.

Figure 6-21. *Return Orders–related list*

   c.   As shown in Figure 6-22, fill in all the relevant fields.

Case: Enter the case number if a case is linked with the return order.

For Account and Contact lookup, add the customer or contact information related to the return order.

For Product Request, if not autopopulated, enter an associated product request. For example, if a mobile worker is returning an unused item, select the related product request that the product was intended to fulfill.

For the Returned By field, select the user returning the items.

For the source and destination locations, enter from and to locations, such as returning items back from Warehouse B to Warehouse A.

Enter a shipment type, an address, and the date the returned products are expected to arrive at the destination location.

Ship From Address represents the location of the items at the start of the return or repair. For example, if a customer is returning an item, enter the customer's address.

   d.   Add a description and click Save. See Figure 6-22.

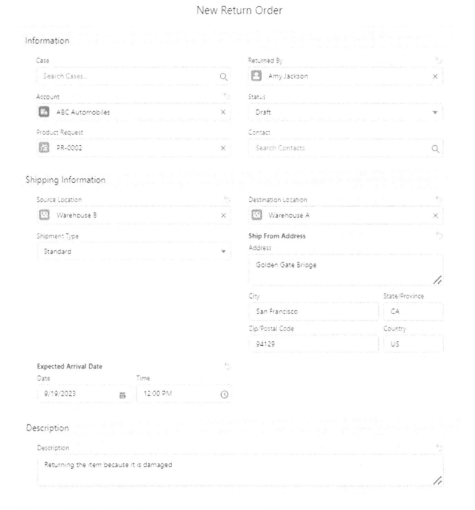

Figure 6-22. *Creating a new return order*

3. Use the Return Order Line Item to track the return for
    a particular item that is sent back as part of a return
    order. Ensure the Return Order Line Item–related list
    is added to the return orders page layout. From the
    setup, navigate to the Object Manager tab, search for
    the Return Order object, and navigate to the page

181

layout. If it's not already added, add the Return Order Line Item–related list to the page layout.

To create a return order line item, follow these steps:

a. While on the Return Order details tab, click the Related tab.

b. Under Return Order Line Item, click New.

c. As shown in Figure 6-23, fill in all the relevant fields.

Based on the part being returned, enter the product, asset, product item, product request line item.

- Products are goods or services your company sells or parts needed to complete the work order.

- Assets are purchased products by customers.

- Product items are products stored at an inventory.

- Product request line items are requested items not in stock.

Under Quantity Returned and Quantity Unit of Measure, enter the number of parts being returned and unit of measure for the returned part.

Select a reason for the return.

Under Processing Plan, specify what should happen to the returned item.

Under Repayment Plan, indicate how the owner should be reimbursed for the return.

If needed, update the source and destination locations. These are inherited from the return order but can be updated.

d. Add a description and click Save.

New Return Order Line Item

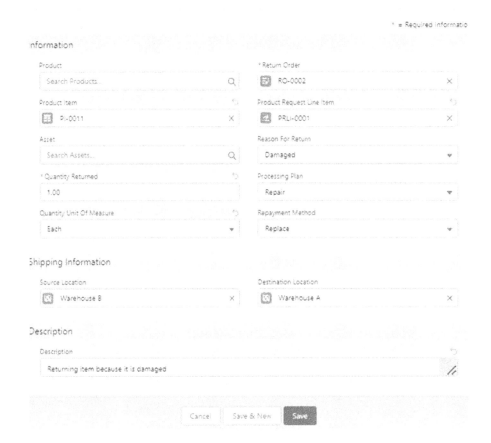

Figure 6-23. *Creating a new return order line item*

Summary

Salesforce Field Service offers a range of inventory management tools that can help organizations effectively manage their inventory levels and ensure that field service technicians have the right parts needed to perform their jobs. Here is an overview of key steps to managing the inventory in Salesforce Field Service:

- Create inventory locations where you will store your inventory, such as warehouses or trucks.

- Create products that you want to track in your inventory.

- Create product items to track products for a specific inventory location. Add the product item transactions-related list to product items to track any movement or changes in the quantity or status of a specific product item.

- Create required products to indicate products that are required to complete a specific service task.

- Create request products to track any products requested by customer or technician.

- Create product transfers to track any products transferred from one location to another.

- Link shipments to product transfers so that your team is always aware of the progress of part transfers.

- Create products consumed to track any products that are used or consumed as part of a service task.

- Create return orders to return products from a customer or technician to the inventory.

Mobile workers can access all the inventory information from their mobile devices. The next chapter provides details of how to set up and use the Salesforce Field Service mobile app.

CHAPTER 7

Extending Field Service to Mobile Devices

Salesforce offers the Field Service mobile app for your workforce to manage their work orders on the go.

In this chapter, we will cover the following:

- Field Service mobile app features

- Setting up the Field Service mobile app

- Customizing the Field Service mobile app

- Using the Field Service mobile app

- The differences between the Salesforce mobile app and the Field Service mobile app capabilities

The Field Service mobile app for Android and iOS provides a one-stop shop for mobile workers with several features that can help your mobile workforce track and complete their work orders hassle free.

Field Service Mobile App Features

The Field Service mobile app allows users to manage and update work orders, track inventory, access customer information, and capture signatures and photos while on the go. Here are some key features of the Salesforce Field Service mobile app:

> *Offline usage*: With offline capabilities, mobile workers can accomplish their tasks even if they have limited or no network connectivity.

> *Push notifications*: Push notifications notify your mobile workforce of upcoming appointments and changes in scheduling.

> *Branding*: The app can be tailored by adding colors and background images.

> *Flexible layouts*: Flexible layouts allow you to pick which record information to show your users.

> *Custom actions*: You can add quick actions to object-specific layouts. These quick actions can be used by mobile users for several tasks such as creating records, updating records or sending messages to contacts, completing work orders, requesting parts, etc. You can add global actions to all page layouts in the app so mobile users can use them from every screen. Salesforce flows can be used to trigger input-based actions.

> *Chatter*: Chatter can be used by mobile workers, dispatchers, team members, and customers to collaborate.

Geolocation tracking: Field service resources can track their current location and get directions to their next job site. This feature uses the device's GPS to provide real-time location data, which can be viewed by supervisors and dispatchers in Salesforce's full site.

Digital service reports: This allows mobile workers to view service reports and get digital signatures from customers all within the app.

Knowledge integration: Knowledge articles such as guidelines, procedures, best practices, and tips can be assigned to work orders or work order line items so workers have access to relevant information within the app.

Site user access: This gives members of your experience builder site custom access to your field service operation.

Find nearby work: Mobile workers can find work orders in their location from the app.

Track inventory: Mobile users can manage their inventory from the app.

Appointment assistant: This lets customers temporarily track a service resource's location when they are en route to the appointment.

App extensions: These let users pass data from the Field Service app to other apps.

Setting Up the Field Service Mobile App

Let's look at how to set up the mobile app.

Minimum Requirements of the Field Service Mobile App

As of July 2023, the minimum requirements for using the Salesforce Field Service Mobile App are as follows:

- *Operating system*: iOS version 15.0 or later or Android version 9.0 or later

- *Network connectivity*: Wi-Fi or cellular data (4G or LTE)

Additionally, the Field Service mobile app may require permissions and settings to be enabled on the device for location services and push notifications in order to work properly.

It's important to note that the device requirements for each Salesforce release and device compatibility always increase per version. Check the help document for the latest updates: `https://help.salesforce.com/s/articleView?id=sf.mfs_requirements.htm&type=5`.

Installing the Field Service Connected App

Before installing the Field Service mobile app, you need to install the managed connected app. The managed package for the connected app is different from the managed package for Field Service, which was covered in Chapter 3. The connected app provides features such as push notifications, geolocation services, and other app settings related to service report generation and app customization.

To install the connected app, follow these steps:

1. Open a new incognito/private browser window and download the connected app at `https://login.salesforce.com/packaging/installPackage.apexp?p0=04t1R0000016Ya8`.

2. On the Salesforce login screen, enter the username and password for the org where you want to install the package; then click Log In.

3. If prompted, paste in the verification code that you receive in your email.

4. Select Install for Admins Only, and then click Install. See Figure 7-1.

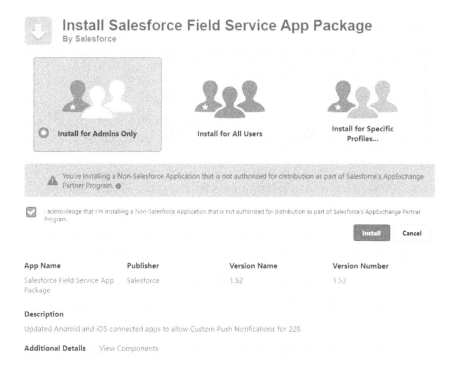

Figure 7-1. *Installing the Field Service Connected app*

5. Approve the request to grant access to third-party websites for geolocation and optimization services.

6. Click Done. You'll be notified by email when the package is installed.

Giving Users Access to the Field Service Mobile App

If you haven't already, assign yourself the Field Service Admin permission to set up mobile workers.

1. From the setup, search for *Users* in the Quick Find box.

2. Click your name.

3. Click Permission Set Assignments under your name.

4. Look for Field Service Admin Permission and assign it to yourself.

Service resources can use the Field Service mobile app only when they have the Field Service Mobile license. To assign mobile licenses to the service resources, follow these steps:

1. Navigate to the app launcher and select the Field Service admin app.

2. Click Field Service Settings.

3. On the Getting Started page, click Go to Guided Setup.

4. Click Create Service Resources.

5. Select User and then Service Territory and click Add.

6. Once the user is added, click the mobile icon in the
    Licenses column to assign the Field Service Mobile
    license and permissions to the service resources.
    See Figure 7-2.

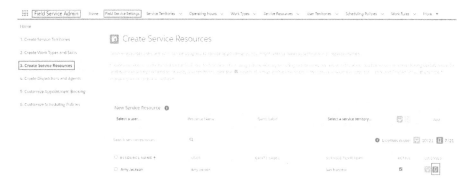

Figure 7-2. *Assigning mobile licenses to service resources*

Assigning Service Record Access

Update the sharing setting so that mobile workers can view their service
resource record in the mobile app.

1. Navigate to the Service Resources tab from the app
    launcher.

2. Go to the All Service Resources list view and click
    the service resource name. See Figure 7-3.

Figure 7-3. *Service resource record sharing*

3.   Click Sharing and choose Read Only.

4.   Click Save.

Note   Users can be given access to a record outside of the organization's defaults or sharing rules by using the Sharing button. The Sharing button is visible only when your sharing model is either Private or Public Read Only for a type of record or related record.

Installing the Field Service Mobile App

To install the app, follow these steps:

1.   Search for *Salesforce Field Service* in the Google Play Store or the iOS App Store on your mobile device and download it.

2.   Once the app is downloaded, tap it to launch it. Approve any requests to let the app do the following:

     •   Send you notifications.

     •   Access your basic information.

- Always access your location. This will be used in the app's mapping functionality and geolocation tracking for scheduling. Your location is tracked when you're using the app and when it's running in the background. If the app isn't running in the background or you're logged out, your location isn't tracked.

- Access your camera.

3. Log in to Salesforce from the app.

4. If prompted, create a passcode for an added level of security.

5. If your Salesforce admin allows logins only through a company-specific login URL such as `mycompany.my.salesforce.com`, you must log in with a custom domain. Click Use Custom Domain to enter a custom domain, as shown in Figure 7-4.

Figure 7-4. *Field Service mobile app login*

6. To specify the production or sandbox org, click
    the gear icon in the top-right corner of the login
    screen and choose the Salesforce org, as shown in
    Figure 7-5.

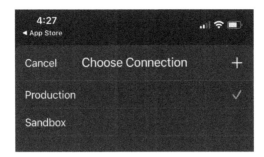

Figure 7-5. *Choosing the Salesforce org*

Customizing the Field Service Mobile App by User Profile

Multiple user profiles, including those of contractors, managers, and other app users, may exist in a business. You can customize the Field Service mobile app according to different user profiles.

1. Switch back to the Salesforce full site.

2. From the setup, in the Quick Find box, search and select Field Service Mobile Settings.

3. Click New to create the new field service mobile settings for the profile.

4. Enter the name and developer name. You can also clone existing Field Service mobile settings. See Figure 7-6.

Figure 7-6. *New Field Service mobile settings*

5. Click Save.

6. Click Assign to Profiles in the upper-right corner.

7. Select a profile and click Change Assignment.

8. Select the Field Service Mobile Settings and click Save. See Figure 7-7.

Assign Field Service Mobile Settings to Profiles

Profile Selected : Contract Manager , Customer Community Login User

* Field Service Mobile Settings

Field Service Mobile App For Other Profiles   ▼

Cancel   Save

Figure 7-7. *Aligning Field Service mobile settings to profiles*

Branding the Field Service Mobile App

As an admin, you can customize the user interface for the Field Service mobile app by choosing from a wide range of colors.

To choose colors, follow these steps:

1. From the Salesforce full site, navigate to the setup.

2. In the Quick Find box, search for and select Field Service Mobile Settings.

3. Click the drop-down list next to Field Service Mobile Settings and click Show Details.

4. In the Branding Colors section, choose the hex colors according to your business needs. See Figure 7-8.

Figure 7-8. *Field Service mobile app brand colors*

Tracking Service Resource Geolocation

This feature can be used to track service resource locations from the Field Service mobile app where the app uploads the geolocation of the app users to Salesforce at regular intervals.

To track service resource geolocation, follow these steps:

1. From the Salesforce full site, navigate to the setup.

2. In the Quick Find box, search for and select Field Service Mobile Settings.

3. Click the drop-down list next to Field Service Mobile Settings and click Show Details.

4. In the Additional Settings section, fill in the following fields:

   • *Collect Service Resource Geolocation History*: Select this field to allow data collection.

- *Geolocation Update Frequency in Minutes*: This determines how frequently geolocation is updated when the app is running in the foreground for both Android and iOS devices.

- *Geolocation Update Frequency in Minutes (Background Mode)*: This determines how frequently geolocation is updated when the app is running in the background on Android devices. For iOS, because of the background mode device limitation, when the app is running in the background, the geolocation is updated only about every five minutes when the device moves 500 meters or more from its previous geolocation. When the app is running in the foreground, geolocation is updated as specified in the Geolocation Update Frequency in Minutes and Geolocation Accuracy fields.

- *Geolocation Accuracy*: This determines the accuracy of the geolocation data collected when the app is running in the foreground. You can choose between the following values:

  Fine: 10 meters

  Medium: 100 meters

  Coarse: 1 kilometer

- *Geolocation Accuracy (Background Mode)*: This determines the accuracy of the geolocation data collected when the app is running in the background. You can choose between the following values:

Medium: 100 meters.

Coarse: 1 kilometer.

Very Coarse: The app does not request geolocation data, and geolocation coordinates are updated only when another app requests geolocation. The accuracy of the geolocation data is determined by the application that initiates the geolocation request. See Figure 7-9.

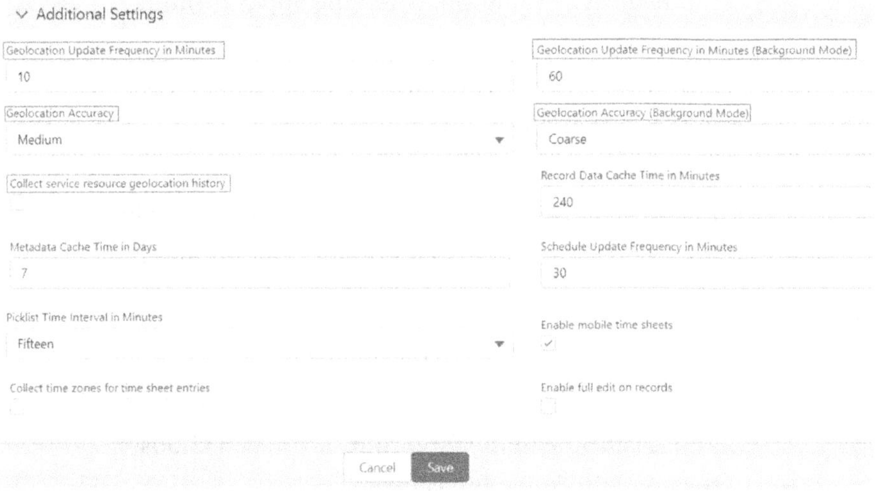

Figure 7-9. *Tracking service resource geolocation*

To enable geolocation tracking, the service resource record access level should be Read/Write.

1. Navigate to the Service Resources tab from the app launcher.

2. Go to the All Service Resources list view and click the service resource name.

3. Click Sharing and choose the Read/Write
   access level.

4. Click Save.

Excluding Specific Service Resources from Geolocation Tracking

Optionally, individual mobile users can turn off location tracking for the Field Service mobile app from the operating system settings on their phone. If you want to exclude specific service resources from the geolocation tracking, such as when not all members of your workforce are legally protected against geolocation tracking, you can do so using permission sets.

Follow these steps to create a permission set to exclude users from the geolocation tracking:

1. From the Salesforce full site, navigate to the setup.

2. In the Quick Find box, enter **Permission Sets** and
   then select Permission Sets.

3. Click New and create a permission set to exclude
   users from geolocation tracking.

4. Enter a label, and under the license, select Field
   Service Mobile.

5. Click Save.

6. Under System Permissions for this permission
   set, click Edit and select Exclude Technician from
   Geolocation Tracking, as shown in Figure 7-10.

7. Click Save.

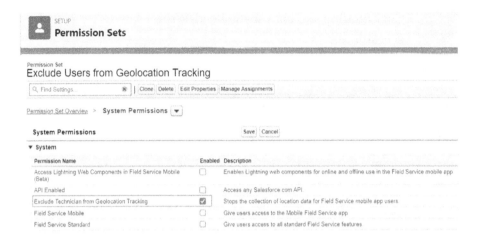

Figure 7-10. Excluding users from geolocation tracking

From Manage Assignments, assign the permission set to the users you want to exclude from the geolocation tracking.

Offline Priming in the Field Service Mobile App

Offline priming makes sure that even if Internet connectivity is lost, a mobile worker has access to all the data they need. Data related to the user's service appointments is automatically downloaded when the user logs into the mobile app. Priming can slow down if there is a huge amount of data to download. If a network error occurs during priming, an error message appears, and priming stops. When you regain connectivity, use the offline priming UI to resync your data. To sync data from your mobile app, follow the steps in this section.

Log in to your Field Service mobile app, click the profile icon in the navigation bar, click the gear icon for Settings, click Data Sync, and then click Sync.

Mobile users see a notification in the top navigation bar if the app goes offline. Changes made while the app is offline are added to the pending uploads queue in the order they occur.

You can speed up the process of offline priming. By default, the mobile app primes your phone with all service appointments for 45 days before and after the current date. You can reduce this date range to speed up the download.

1. Switch back to the Salesforce full site.

2. From setup, in the Quick Find box, search for and select Field Service Mobile Settings.

3. Click the drop-down list next to Field Service Mobile Settings and click Show Details.

4. Under Customization, update Future Days in the Date Picker and Past Days in the Date Picker fields and click Save. See Figure 7-11.

Figure 7-11. *Speeding up offline priming*

Push Notifications for the Field Service Mobile App

Push notifications can be used to notify your mobile workforce about approaching appointments or schedule changes.

To set up push notifications, follow these steps:

1. From the Salesforce full site, navigate to the setup.

2. In the Quick Find box, search and select Field Service Settings.

3. Under Notifications, select Enable Notifications.

4. Under Sharing, select all three checkboxes. See Figure 7-12.

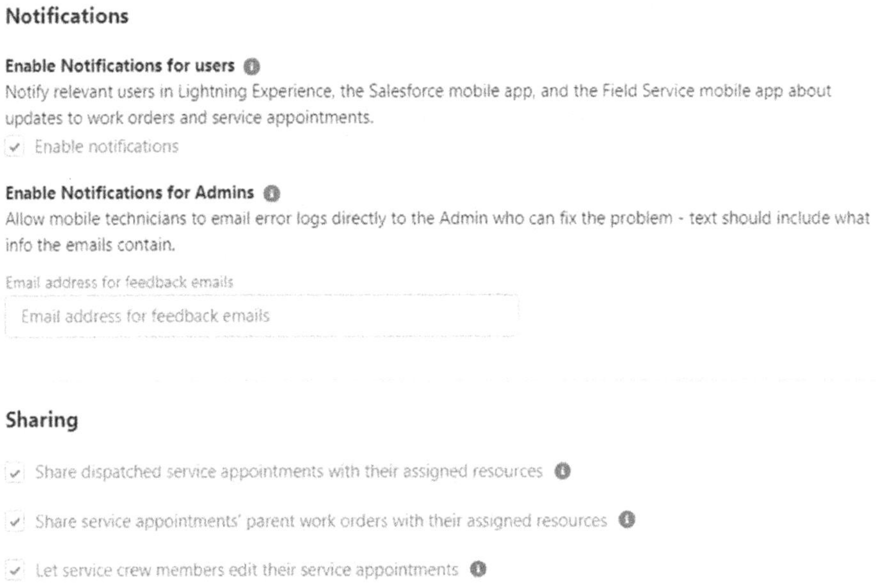

Notifications

Enable Notifications for users ⓘ
Notify relevant users in Lightning Experience, the Salesforce mobile app, and the Field Service mobile app about updates to work orders and service appointments.

☑ Enable notifications

Enable Notifications for Admins ⓘ
Allow mobile technicians to email error logs directly to the Admin who can fix the problem - text should include what info the emails contain.

Email address for feedback emails

| Email address for feedback emails |

Sharing

☑ Share dispatched service appointments with their assigned resources ⓘ

☑ Share service appointments' parent work orders with their assigned resources ⓘ

☑ Let service crew members edit their service appointments ⓘ

Figure 7-12. *Enabling push notifications*

5. Click Save.

To choose when appointment notifications are sent, follow these steps:

1. From the Salesforce full site, navigate to the setup.

2. In the Quick Find box, search for and select Field Service Mobile Settings.

3. Click the drop-down list next to Field Service Mobile
    Settings and click Show Details.

4. In the Customization section, select "Send
    appointment notifications on dispatch" and "Send
    appointment notifications on assignment."

    - *Send appointment notifications on dispatch*: With
      this option, users are notified when the status of
      the case is changed to Dispatched and when their
      assignment is changed or withdrawn.

    - *Send appointment notifications on assignment*:
      With this option, users are notified when they're
      assigned to a service appointment and when
      their assignment is changed or removed. They're
      not notified when they're dispatched for the
      appointment. See Figure 7-13.

Figure 7-13. *Sending appointment notifications on dispatch and*
assignment

Even if the service resources change or are removed from the service
appointment after dispatchment or assignment, they will still receive
notifications. Selecting both these options will allow notifications when
the service appointment is dispatched and assigned. If neither option is
selected, no service appointment notifications are sent.

Setting Up Automatic Status Changes

Mobile workers need not change the status of a service appointment manually because the Field Service app can automatically track status changes for them.

Automatic status changes occur three times based on the location and time.

- Starting travel

- Arriving on-site

- Completing an appointment

To set up automatic status changes, follow these steps:

1. From the Salesforce full site, navigate to the setup.

2. In the Quick Find box, search for and select Field Service Mobile Settings.

3. Click the drop-down list next to Field Service Mobile Settings and click Show Details.

4. In the Automatic Status Change section, do the following:

    - Select a mode.

      Manual: This requires the mobile user to cancel or confirm the change.

      Timed: This requires the mobile user to cancel or confirm the change. If no action is taken, the status changes when the timer ends.

      Automatic: The mobile user need not cancel or confirm the change. The user worker is informed about the change after it happens.

- Select the status that should be assigned when the mobile user is traveling, is on-site, and has completed the appointment under Traveling Status, Onsite Status, and Completed Status fields, respectively.

- Enter the service appointment radius (100–5,000 meters) when the status change should trigger using the Radius in Meters field.

- Enter the amount of time (1–60 minutes) before an appointment's scheduled start time or actual end time when the status change should trigger under the Time Limit in Minutes field.

- Enter the duration (10–600 seconds) that the timer is visible under the Cancellation or Dismissal Timer in Seconds. After this time, the status changes automatically and can't be canceled. This setting is only for Timed mode. See Figure 7-14.

Figure 7-14. *Setting up automatic status changes*

5. Click Save.

Note   To set up automatic status changes, mobile users should set the location permission to Always on their device.

Creating Global Actions

To make routine tasks easy for your team members, you can add global actions to the mobile app. These global actions can be accessed from any screens in the mobile app as they are added to the publisher layout and not to object-specific page layouts.

To create a global action, follow these steps:

1. From the Salesforce full site, navigate to the setup.

2. In the Quick Find box, enter **Actions** and then select Global Actions.

3. Click New Action.

4. Select the action type Create a Record. The Field Service mobile app only supports this action type.

5. Select the target object and standard label type you want to create a record for.

6. Enter the name, description, and success message. See Figure 7-15.

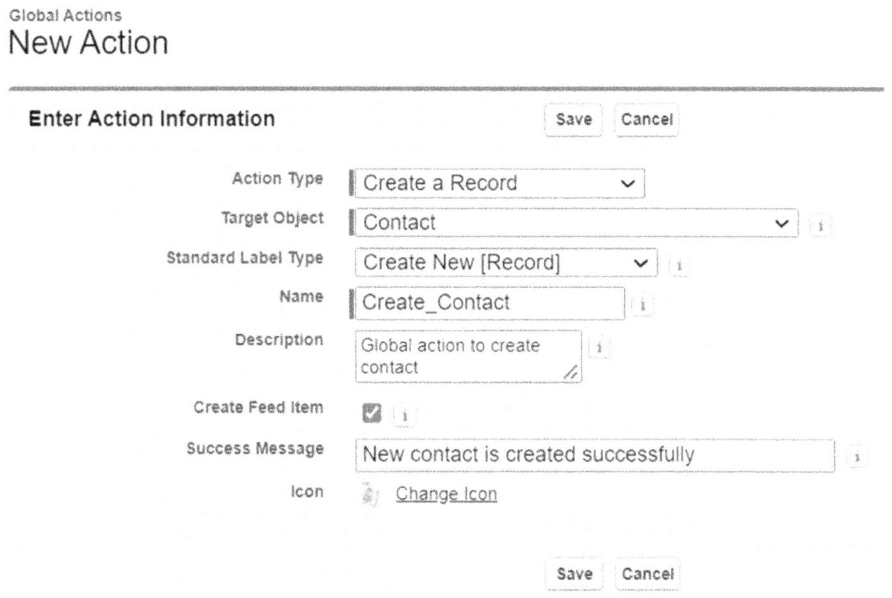

Global Actions
New Action

Enter Action Information   Save   Cancel

Action Type	Create a Record ⌄
Target Object	Contact ⌄ ⓘ
Standard Label Type	Create New [Record] ⌄ ⓘ
Name	Create_Contact ⓘ
Description	Global action to create contact ⓘ
Create Feed Item	☑ ⓘ
Success Message	New contact is created successfully ⓘ
Icon	🖼 Change Icon

Save   Cancel

Figure 7-15. *Creating a global action*

7. Click Save. On saving, you should be automatically
    navigated to the action layout. Add the relevant
    fields to the layout and save.

Once the global action is created, it should be added to the publisher
layout for visibility.

1. In the Quick Find box, enter **Publisher Layout** and
    then select Publisher Layouts.

2. Click Edit next to the publisher layout.

3. Drag an action from the Quick Actions list and drop
    it under Quick Actions in the Salesforce Classic
    Publisher section.

4. Drag an action from the Mobile & Lightning Actions
    and drop it under the Salesforce Mobile and
    Lightning Experience Actions section.

5.   Click Save. See Figure 7-16.

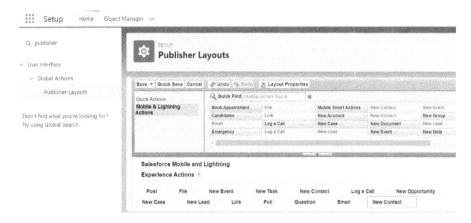

Figure 7-16. *Adding a global action to the publisher layout*

Creating Quick Actions

You can add quick actions to the mobile app to help your team cut down on the number of steps and perform tasks quickly. Unlike global actions, quick actions are added to the object-specific page layout instead of the publisher layout. In the mobile app, quick actions are visible only on the object record. For example, you can add a Create Opportunity action and add it to the contact page layout to let users create an opportunity from any contact record in the mobile app.

To create a quick action, follow these steps:

1.   From the setup, navigate to the Object Manager tab and select the object.

2.   Click Buttons, Links, and Actions on the left side.

3.   Click New Action.

4.   Select the action type, target object, and standard label type.

5. Enter the name, description, and success message.
    See Figure 7-17.

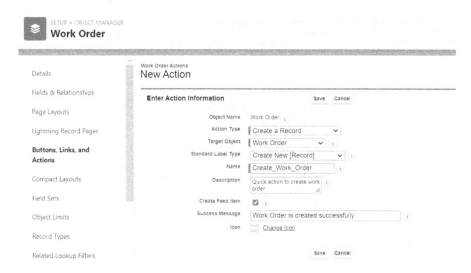

Figure 7-17. *Creating a quick action*

6. Click Save.

7. Add any related fields to the quick action layout
    and click Save. You can also predefine values
    for the fields under Predefined Field Values. See
    Figure 7-18.

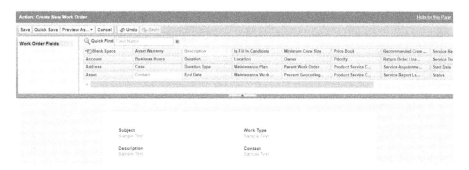

Figure 7-18. *Adding fields to the quick action*

Once created, a quick action should be added to the object page layout for visibility.

1. Click Page Layouts on the left side.

2. Click Edit next to the page layout.

3. Drag an action from the Quick Actions list and drop it under Quick Actions in the Salesforce Classic Publisher section.

4. Drag an action from the Mobile & Lightning Actions and drop it in the Salesforce Mobile and Lightning Experience Actions section.

5. Click Save.

You can add actions to child objects such as work order line items as well. Global actions and quick actions will appear in the mobile app as well as the full Salesforce site.

Building Flows for the Field Service Mobile App

You can guide your users by using mobile flows to view information, create and update records, and trigger input-based actions.

Let's create a flow that tracks a checklist of things to do when the workers reach the site. Workers can check off each task as they complete it.

To create a flow, follow these steps:

1. In the Quick Find box, enter **flows** and then select Flows.

2. Click New Flow.

3. On the All + Templates tab, select Field Service Mobile Flow. See Figure 7-19.

Figure 7-19. *Creating a Field Service mobile flow*

4. Click Create.

5. Change the layout from Auto-Layout to Free-Form
    in the upper-right corner.

6. Drag Screen from the palette to the flow.

7. Under Screen Properties, enter the label, API name,
    and description for your flow.

8. Drag and drop a checkbox from the Components
    tab. Drop in as many checkbox components
    as needed.

9. Enter the label and API name for all the checkboxes.
    See Figure 7-20.

Figure 7-20. *Adding a checkbox to the flow*

10. Click Done.

11. While in the flow builder, connect the start element and screen element by clicking the circle at the bottom of the Start element and dragging the line to the circle at the bottom of the Screen element, as shown in Figure 7-21.

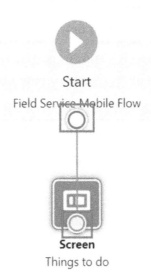

Figure 7-21. *Connecting flow elements*

12. Click Save.

13. Enter the flow label and flow API name.

14. Click Save and then Activate.

In the next topic, you will learn how to add the flow to the Field Service mobile app using app extensions.

Creating App Extensions for the Field Service Mobile App

App extensions allow users to transfer data from the Field Service app to another app.

To create an app extension, follow these steps:

1. From the Salesforce full site, navigate to the setup.

2. In the Quick Find box, search for and select Field Service Mobile Settings.

3. Click the drop-down list next to Field Service Mobile Settings and click Show Details.

4. In the App Extensions section, click New.

5. Enter the following fields:

   • *Field Service Mobile Settings*: This field is autopopulated with the name of the Field Service mobile settings.

   • *Label*: The label as it appears to users in the app.

   • *Type*: Select the app extension type.

     iOS: This type will be visible only on iOS devices.

     Android: This type will be visible only on iOS devices.

Flow: This type refers to flows. The Field Service mobile flow falls under this category. To connect the flow created in the previous topic to the Field Service mobile app, select this type.

Lightning App: This type refers to an app that is exposed in Salesforce for Android or iOS.

- *Name*: This is the app extension's name.

- *Scoped To Object Types*: Scoping an app extension to an object lets users activate that app extension from records of the specified object. Enter the object's API name such as ServiceAppointment (the service appointment object's API name).

- *Launch Value*: This is the value used to launch the app or flow. If the type is Flow, then the launch value is the API name of the flow, while if the type is Lightning App, the launch value is the name of the tab in Salesforce for iOS and Salesforce for Android.

- *Installation URL*: This is the URL that takes the user to the app install location, such as the App Store or Google Play.

6. Click Save. See Figure 7-22.

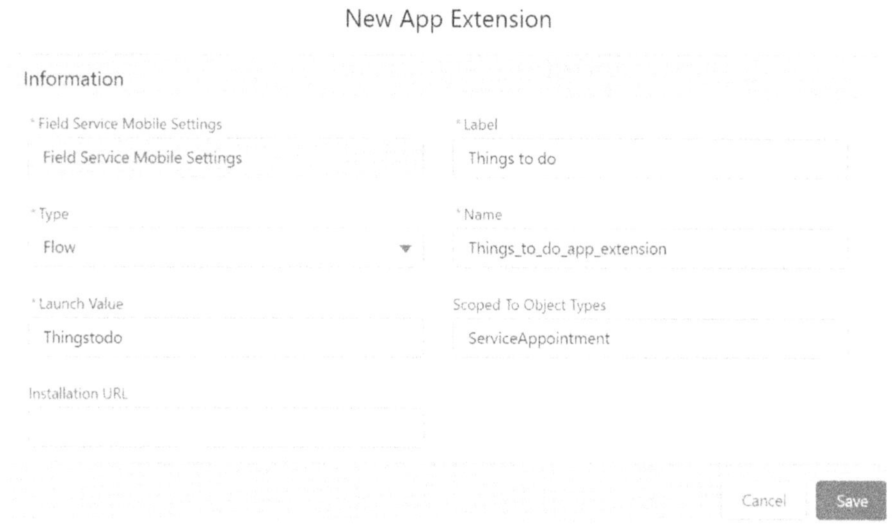

New App Extension

Information

* Field Service Mobile Settings

Field Service Mobile Settings

* Type

Flow ▼

* Launch Value

Thingstodo

Installation URL

* Label

Things to do

* Name

Things_to_do_app_extension

Scoped To Object Types

ServiceAppointment

Cancel   Save

Figure 7-22. *Creating a new app extension*

Given that we included the service appointment object in the Scoped To Object Types field, the flow is now associated with the Field Service mobile app and will be accessible under the service appointment record.

Order of Actions

By clicking the Actions button on the work order overview screen from the Field Service mobile app, users can see actions in the following order:

1. The Create Service Report action is displayed when the Service Appointment page layouts have a Service Reports–related list. If you have configured an alternate service closure flow, then this action will not be visible.

2. The Custom App Extensions and Flows scoped to the object types Service Appointment and Work Order Objects are sorted alphanumerically and displayed at the top of the section.

3. After App Extensions and Flows, Salesforce Classic Publisher Quick Actions are displayed in the order of the page's layout (Android only).

4. After Quick Actions, Edit Work Order, Edit Work Order Line Item, and Edit Service Appointment are displayed.

5. App extensions and flows not scoped to an object are shown at the bottom of the page layout.

Using the App

The following sections show how to use the app.

Logging In to the Field Service Mobile App

Once you have provided users with the Field Service Mobile license, they can download the Salesforce Field Service mobile app from the iOS App Store or Google Play Store and log in using the following steps:

1. Click Use Custom Domain.

2. Enter your Salesforce org's company-specific My Domain name. Enter just the domain name. The system will add *.my.salesforce.com.*

3. Click Continue.

4. Enter the username and password and click Log In.

5. Click Allow to grant access.

Touring the App

Once you have successfully logged in, you should see the following items on your screen:

- *Calendar*: You can view appointments for various days by selecting the calendar icon in the top-right corner. There are appointments scheduled for the date, as indicated by the tiny circle above it. See Figure 7-23.

Figure 7-23. *Calendar*

- *Map*: A map is an interactive way to view the service appointment, ETA, driving directions, etc. To get travel instructions and additional information about the service appointment, zoom in on the map by clicking it. See Figure 7-24.

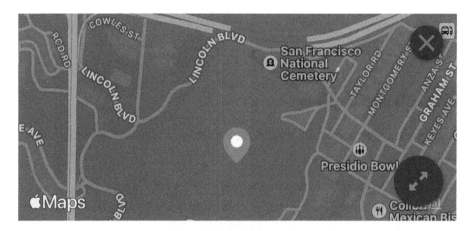

Figure 7-24. *Map*

- *Service appointments*: Tap the service appointment to
  see more information about it. See Figure 7-25.

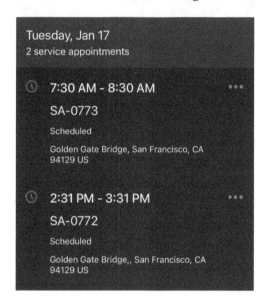

Figure 7-25. *Service appointments*

- *Actions*: Click the Actions button to view any quick actions, global actions, or flows. See Figure 7-26.

Figure 7-26. *Actions*

- *Navigation bar*: View your daily schedule, the inventory needed for your service appointments, system or dispatcher notifications, your profile, and more. To view additional information about each icon, tap it. See Figure 7-27.

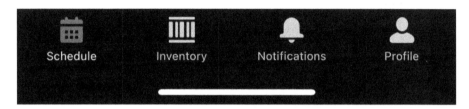

Figure 7-27. *Navigation bar*

Tap the service appointment, and you can see the work order number and subject at the top of the screen. See Figure 7-28.

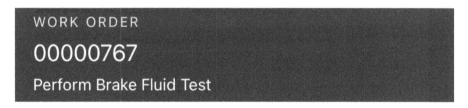

Figure 7-28. *Work order number*

Subtabs: These are Overview, Details, Related, and Feed. See
Figure 7-29.

OVERVIEW   DETAILS   RELATED   FEED

Figure 7-29. *Subtabs*

1. *Overview*: You can see a map and get directions for
   the site location. On scrolling down, you can see
   the contact information and asset service history.
   You can create a service report for the service
   appointment from this tab.

2. *Details*: You can see all the work order information
   such as service territory, description, work type, etc.
   See Figure 7-30.

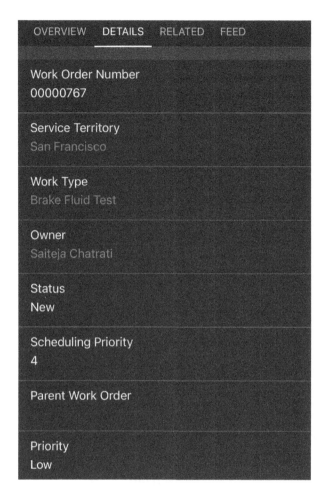

Figure 7-30. *Work order details*

3. *Related*: You can see items related to the work
   order such as the work order line items, service
   appointments, skill requirements, and child work
   orders. See Figure 7-31.

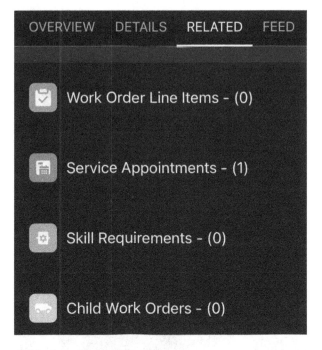

Figure 7-31. *Work order–related lists*

4. *Feed*: Users can post comments or communicate
    with other team members. For example, a user can
    post here if more information is needed from the
    dispatcher. You can share screenshots or use @ to
    notify individual users. See Figure 7-32.

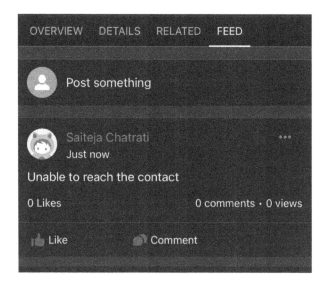

Figure 7-32. *Feed*

Creating a Service Report

The service report includes a summary of the work order or work order line item. Mobile users can create service reports from the Field Service mobile app.

Admins will have to ensure the following steps are completed in the full Salesforce site:

1. Ensure service report templates are configured as specified in Chapter 5.

2. If not already added, add the Service Reports–related list to the Service Appointment page layout.

3. Ensure the Work Type field is added to the work order and work order line item page layouts, and make sure mobile users have permissions to view it.

225

4. Ensure the Service Report Template field is added
    to the work type page layout. Navigate to the Work
    Types tab from the app launcher and select a service
    report template for each work type. When mobile
    users generate the service report from their mobile,
    the template specified on the work type related
    to the work order or work order line item will be
    selected. If you do not specify the template, the
    default service report template is selected.

Once these steps are configured by admins, mobile users can create a
service report in the Field Service mobile app by following these steps:

1. Navigate to the work order, work order line item, or
    service appointment.

2. On the Overview subtab, click the Actions icon.

3. Click the Create Service Report action. See
    Figure 7-33.

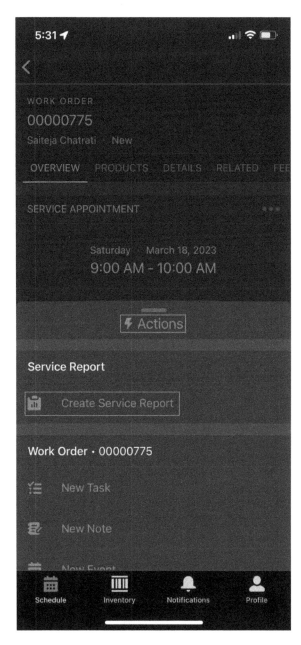

Figure 7-33. *Creating service reports in the Field Service mobile app*

4. If the service resource template includes a signature section, you will be prompted to get the signature; otherwise, the confirm option appears. If no signatures are needed, you can confirm and generate the service report.

5. If signatures are needed, click Get Signature, select Get Signature Default, click Sign & Confirm, get the signee's name and signature, click Save, and click Generate Service Report. See Figure 7-34.

Figure 7-34. *Getting a signature on the service report*

Once the service report is generated, it will be attached to the work order, work order line item, or service appointment. It is saved under the Service Reports–related list.

Managing the Inventory in the Field Service Mobile App

With inventory management supported on both Android and iOS, you can give your mobile workers the ability to manage the inventory from within the mobile app.

Mobile workers can view and update their inventory, log product consumption, create product requests, and add required products by clicking the Inventory icon in the navigation bar at the bottom of the app.

Users can utilize the mobile device to view the inventory that is currently available. For service resources to view the inventory, they should be associated with the mobile inventory location. They must have at least read access to product items or product requests.

Location is a physical area where products are stored. Types of locations could be warehouse, sites, or vehicles. As field service employees frequently transport products in their vehicles, you can define a field location type to reflect their inventory, such as a vehicle.

To define a location and location type, follow these steps:

1. Switch back to the Salesforce full site.

2. Navigate to the Locations tab from the app launcher.

3. Click the New button to create a location.

4. Enter a location name and location type.

5. Check the Inventory Location and Mobile Location checkboxes. See Figure 7-35.

Figure 7-35. *Creating a location*

6.   Click Save.

Now to assign this location to the service resource, follow these steps:

1.   If it's not already added, add the Location field to
the Service Resource page layout.

From the setup, navigate to the Object Manager
tab, search for the Service Resource object, navigate
to the page layout, and add the Location field to
the layout.

2. Navigate to the Service Resources tab from the app launcher.

3. Go to the All Service Resources list view and click the service resource name.

4. Click Edit in the upper-right corner. Expand the small drop-down arrow to see the Edit action.

5. In the location lookup field, search for the location and click Save. See Figure 7-36.

Figure 7-36. *Service resource location assignment*

John Doe can now see the inventory tab on his mobile device because his service resource record is linked to the location.

Service resources can manage product items associated with their mobile inventory location from the mobile app.

To let service resources add products consumed or products required records, add these related lists to the work order or work order line item page layouts from the full Salesforce site.

Adding Resource Absences

Service resources can indicate their absences by doing the following:

1. Navigate to the Profile icon and click the Add icon next to Resource Absences, as shown in Figure 7-37.

2. Choose the type of absence: Break or Non Availability.

3. Enter all the details and click Save. See Figure 7-37.

Figure 7-37. *Adding a resource absence*

Adding Timesheets

Service resources can submit timesheets from the Field Service mobile app b following these steps:

1. Ensure timesheets are configured as specified in the Logging Timesheets topic in Chapter 5.

2. From the Field Service mobile app, navigate to the Profile icon and click the clock icon in the upper-left corner.

3. Under Current Time Sheets, the timesheet for the current week will be visible. If you have set up the time sheet templates as covered in Chapter 5, the time sheet will be automatically created. Click the small drop-down next to the current time sheets and select Past Time Sheets to see the previously added timesheets. See Figure 7-38.

Figure 7-38. *Viewing timesheets*

4. Tap a timesheet to log hours for each day. You
   can track individual tasks for the day as timesheet
   entries. As shown in Figure 7-39, click the plus icon
   to add a timesheet entry for that day. Enter the
   subject, start time, and end time. The total hours
   will be automatically calculated. Optionally fill in
   the other fields. Click the plus icon again to add

another timesheet entry under the timesheet. Click the three dots next to the time sheet entry to edit or delete the timesheet entry.

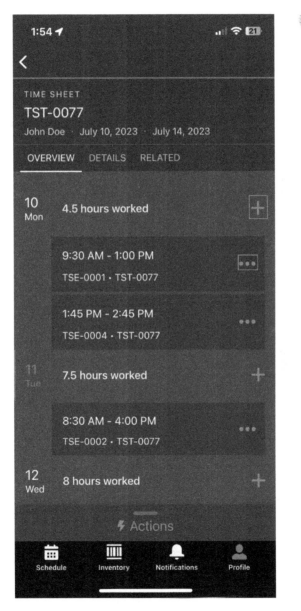

Figure 7-39. Adding timesheet entries

5. Once you're done adding timesheets for all the days, navigate back to the previous screen and click Submit to submit them for approvals. If you have set up an approval process, then the timesheet will be sent to the manager for approval.

Understanding the Differences Between the Salesforce Mobile App and Field Service Mobile App

The Salesforce mobile app and Salesforce Field Service mobile app are two different mobile applications that serve different purposes. Table 7-1 lists some key differences between the two.

Table 7-1. *Difference Between Salesforce Mobile App and Field Service Mobile App*

	Salesforce Mobile App	Salesforce Field Service Mobile App
Functionality	The Salesforce mobile app is a comprehensive mobile app that provides access to all Salesforce modules, including sales, service, and marketing, and allows users to manage their accounts, contacts, opportunities, and cases.	The Salesforce Field Service mobile app is focused specifically on field service operations and provides functionality tailored to the needs of technicians and field workers, such as managing work orders, tracking inventory and assets, and accessing customer information.

(continued)

Table 7-1. (*continued*)

	Salesforce Mobile App	Salesforce Field Service Mobile App
Target audience	Designed for all Salesforce users, including sales reps, service agents, marketers, and executives.	Designed specifically for technicians and field workers who are involved in field service operations.
User interface	The user interface of Salesforce mobile app is designed to be more general-purpose and flexible.	The Salesforce Field Service mobile app has a more specific user interface that is tailored to the needs of technicians and field workers.
Integration:	The Salesforce mobile app can integrate with a wider range of Salesforce products.	The Salesforce Field Service mobile app is specifically designed to integrate with the Salesforce Field Service Lightning product.

While both the applications are designed distinctly, they can be integrated with other Salesforce products and third-party applications.

Summary

Salesforce Field Service is a mobile app different from the Salesforce mobile app that allows field service resources to access and update work orders and customer information on the go. Here are some steps to get started with Salesforce Field Service Mobile.

As an admin, you can do the following:

- Install Field Service connected app. Connected app managed package is different from the Field Service managed package. Installing the connected app will allow features such as push notifications, geolocation services, and other app settings related to service report generation and app customization.

- Give users access to the Field Service mobile app. Service resources will be needing the Field Service Mobile App license to utilize the app.

- Update the sharing setting on the service resource record so that mobile users can view their service resource record in the mobile app.

- From the Field Service Mobile Settings, customize the Field Service mobile app for multiple user profiles such as contractors, supervisors, and other app users.

- Brand the app by utilizing the color palette.

- Configure the Field Service mobile settings to ensure the Field Service mobile app regularly uploads the geolocation of the app to Salesforce.

- Speed up the process of offline priming. By default, the mobile app primes your phone with all service appointments for 45 days before and after the current date. You can reduce this date range to speed up the download.

- Enable push notifications to notify your mobile workforce about approaching appointments or schedule changes.

- Set up automatic status change so that service resources need not change the status of the service appointment manually.

- Configure global and quick actions to give your team members easy access to common tasks. Global actions can be accessed from any screen in the mobile app, while quick actions are visible only on the object record.

- Configure mobile flows to view information, create and update records, and trigger input-based actions.

- Configure app extensions to allow users to transfer data from the Field Service app to another app.

As a service resource, you can do the following:

- Install the Field Service mobile app from the iOS App Store or Google Play Store.

- Log in to the app to view the service appointments, update the information, manage inventory, create service reports, add the resources absences, and log timesheets.

CHAPTER 8

Field Service Deployment, Testing, and Analytics

Deploying Salesforce Field Service can be a time-consuming and complex process that requires careful planning, strong project management, and close collaboration between the implementation team and key stakeholders. With a well-executed deployment, organizations can realize the full benefits of Salesforce Field Service, including improved operational efficiency, enhanced customer satisfaction, and increased revenue growth.

This chapter will cover the following:

- Best practices for the deployment and testing processes to ensure a smooth and efficient transition

- KPIs and analytics to track the overall performance of the Field Service application

- Upcoming trends in Salesforce Field Service

© Saiteja Chatrati 2023
S. Chatrati, *Salesforce Field Service*, https://doi.org/10.1007/978-1-4842-9517-5_8

Deployment Phases

The deployment process for Salesforce Field Service typically involves the following phases:

- Pre-deployment planning

- Implementation and testing

- Post-deployment support

Pre-deployment Planning

The goal of this phase is to ensure that the deployment is well-defined, adequately resourced, and aligned with business needs. The following are some key activities that organizations should consider during the pre-deployment planning phase.

Pre-deployment Documentation

The first step in pre-deployment planning is to document all the key project deliverables.

- *Business requirements document*: This defines the current and future field service processes, key objectives, pain points, goals, and Field Service elements such as service territories, work types, service resources, business scheduling policies, template definitions, mobile app requirements, products, etc.

- *Deployment plan*: This outlines the scope, timelines, rollback plan, and procedures necessary to deploy the Field Service solution to the production environment. This includes identifying any dependencies, defining the order in which components will be deployed, and determining any potential risks and mitigation strategies.

- *Configuration checklist*: Use this checklist as a handy tool to keep track of all the configurations built into the sandbox environment such as custom permissions sets, profiles, fields, skills, assets, inventory, email templates, etc., that need to be deployed to the production. This ensures that no configuration is missed during production deployment.

- *Test plan*: This defines the testing team, test cases, test data, test steps, or test tools used to perform the testing.

Allocate Resources

This includes identifying the project team, defining roles and responsibilities, and establishing a timeline for the deployment. It is also important to identify end users who will be performing the user acceptance testing (UAT).

Identify Potential Issues and Risks

During pre-deployment planning, it is important to identify potential issues and risks that could impact the success of the deployment. This includes technical issues, data quality issues, and user adoption issues. By identifying these risks early on, organizations can create a mitigation plan to address them and reduce the likelihood of project delays or failures.

Budget Planning

Finally, organizations should consider budget planning during the pre-deployment planning phase. This involves estimating the costs associated with the deployment, including hardware, software, licensing, consulting, and training costs. By developing a detailed budget, organizations can ensure that they have the necessary resources to complete the deployment successfully.

Rollout Communication Planning

This is a critical aspect of the deployment process that ensures all the stakeholders are informed and aware of the changes being made to the Salesforce environment. Early and effective communication can help to reduce resistance to change, minimize disruption to business operations, and increase user adoption of the new functionality.

Pre-deployment planning is a critical phase of Salesforce Field Service deployment that sets the foundation for the entire project. By taking the time to document important artifacts, allocate resources, identify potential issues, plan the budget, and effectively communicate the rollout plan, organizations can ensure a smooth and successful deployment of Salesforce Field Service.

Implementation and Testing

It is essential to follow best practices while deploying Salesforce Field Service to production. It is recommended that changes should always be made in a sandbox environment first. Always create a backup of your production environment before deploying, and ensure that all stakeholders are informed about the deployment. Test thoroughly in a sandbox environment before deploying to production, and conduct user acceptance testing to ensure that everything is working as expected.

Here are some key steps to deploy Salesforce Field Service from a sandbox to production:

1. *Prepare the sandbox*: Before deploying Salesforce Field Service to production, you must prepare the sandbox environment. This involves ensuring that the sandbox environment is a copy of your production environment and that all customizations and configurations are up-to-date.

2. *Prepare your data*: Before implementing Salesforce Field Service in production, you must ensure that your data is clean, accurate, and complete. This involves importing data into Salesforce, cleaning up duplicates and inconsistencies, and ensuring that data is structured in a way that is compatible with the Field Service application.

3. *Set up Field Service*: Enable Field Service in your production org. Install and configure the Field Service managed package. This includes setting up scheduling policies, dispatching rules, service territories, and more.

4. *Configure your workforce*: Set up your workforce in Field Service by creating resources (technicians, agents, etc.), defining their skills and availability, and assigning them to service territories.

5. *Configure your assets and inventory*: Define the assets and inventory that your field service team will work with, and set up tracking for these items in Field Service.

6. *Deploying metadata*: This involves using the Salesforce deployment tools, such as change sets or the Metadata API, to migrate components such as flows, approval processes, custom fields, reports, or any other configurations from the sandbox environment to production.

7. *Integrate with other systems*: Connect Field Service to other systems in your IT infrastructure, such as ERP, inventory management, or billing systems, to ensure seamless data exchange.

8. *Test the deployment*: Thoroughly test the solution to ensure that it functions as expected in the production environment. This involves testing the application, conducting user acceptance testing, and verifying that all data and configurations are properly migrated.

Testing and Quality Assurance

Testing Salesforce Field Service is an important step in ensuring that the system is working correctly and meeting the needs of the business. There are several types of testing that can be performed to evaluate the performance of the system.

- *Unit testing*: This involves testing individual components of the system to ensure that they are functioning correctly. This type of testing is typically done by developers and focuses on verifying the functionality of individual pieces of code.

- *Systems integration testing*: This type of testing involves testing how the Field Service system works in conjunction with other systems, such as CRM or ERP systems. It ensures that data is flowing correctly between systems and that the overall system is working as intended.

- *User acceptance testing (UAT)*: This type of testing involves testing the system from the perspective of end users, such as dispatchers and technicians. It ensures that the system is easy to use and meets the needs of the business.

- *Performance testing*: This type of testing evaluates the performance of the system under different conditions, such as high traffic or heavy usage. It ensures that the system can handle the expected load and performs well under normal and peak conditions.

- *Regression testing*: This type of testing involves testing the system after changes have been made to ensure that new functionality has not affected existing functionality. It ensures that the system continues to work as intended and that changes do not introduce new issues.

Field Service Health Check

Salesforce offers a Field Service Health Check tool using which you can test your configuration by running automated tests. The health check typically involves a comprehensive review of the system's configuration and processes to identify areas for improvement.

You can perform two types of validations: general and horizon based.

- *General based*: Use this to confirm that configurations such as scheduling policies and permission sets are correctly set up for your org.

- *Horizon based*: For a given time horizon, service territory, and scheduling policy, this validation checks the service appointments, resources, and territory memberships.

For both the validations, results are categorized as critical tests and important tests. Performance losses may occur right away if a critical test fails, while performance can be negatively impacted by an important test failure, or it can be impacted later due to other customizations.

To run a health check, follow these steps:

1. Navigate to the Field Service admin app from the app launcher.

2. Navigate to the Field Service Settings tab.

3. Click Health Check.

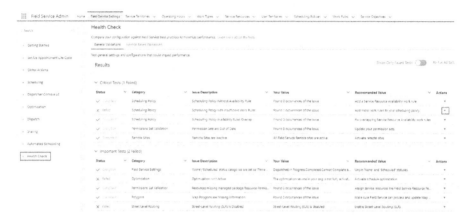

Figure 8-1. *General-based Validation*

On the General Validations tab, you should see both critical and important tests. Green indicates passed tests, while red indicates failed tests. To see more details about the failed tests, click the drop-down next to the failed test and click More Info.

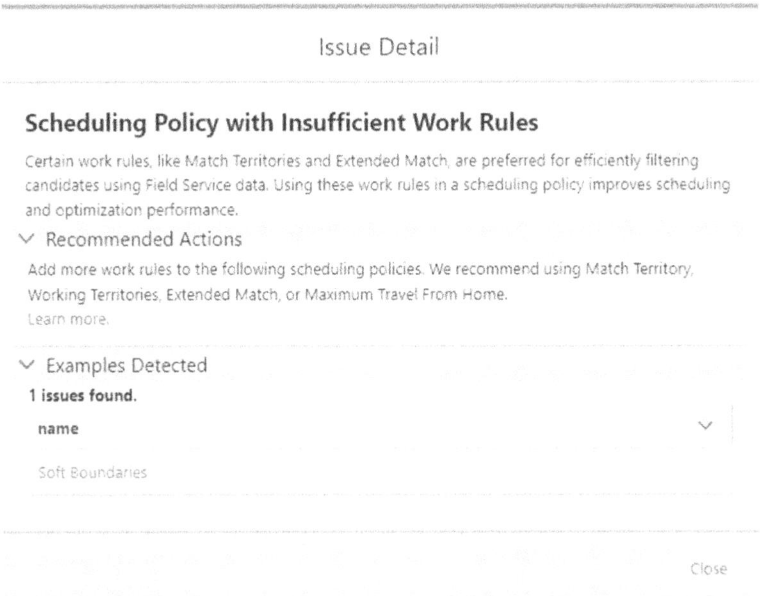

Issue Detail

Scheduling Policy with Insufficient Work Rules

Certain work rules, like Match Territories and Extended Match, are preferred for efficiently filtering candidates using Field Service data. Using these work rules in a scheduling policy improves scheduling and optimization performance.

∨ Recommended Actions

Add more work rules to the following scheduling policies. We recommend using Match Territory, Working Territories, Extended Match, or Maximum Travel From Home.
Learn more.

∨ Examples Detected

1 issues found.

name   ∨

Soft Boundaries

Close

Figure 8-2. *Issue detail*

To fix the issue, follow the recommended actions provided in the issue detail and rerun the tests.

To run horizon-based validation, on the Horizon Based Validation tab, enter values for Horizon Start, Horizon End, Service Territory, Scheduling Policy, and click Run Tests.

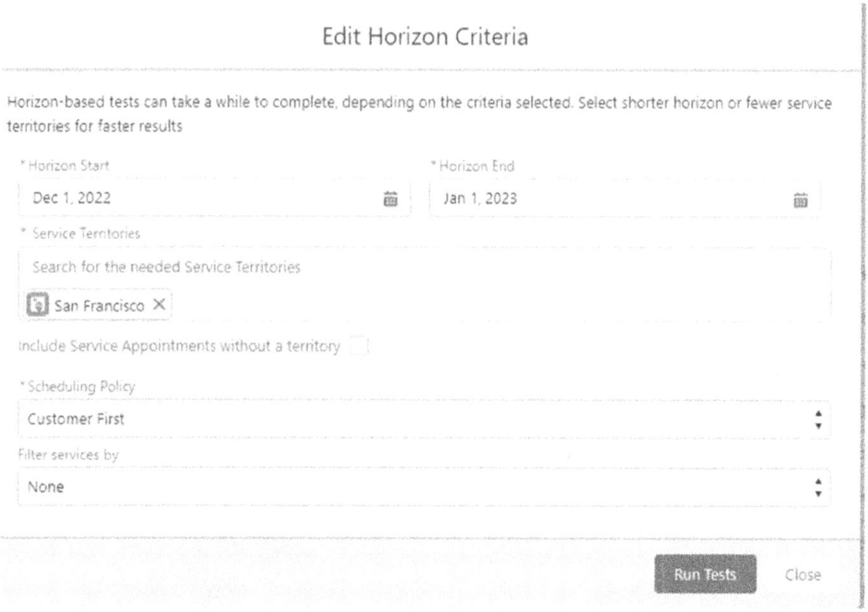

Edit Horizon Criteria

Horizon-based tests can take a while to complete, depending on the criteria selected. Select shorter horizon or fewer service territories for faster results

* Horizon Start

Dec 1, 2022

* Horizon End

Jan 1, 2023

* Service Territories

Search for the needed Service Territories

San Francisco ✕

Include Service Appointments without a territory

* Scheduling Policy

Customer First

Filter services by

None

Run Tests   Close

Figure 8-3. *Horizon-based Validation*

You should see critical and important tests. Click the drop-down next to a failed test to see more information about it. Follow the recommended action to fix the issue.

Post-deployment Support

Once the system is live, ongoing maintenance and updates are required. This phase includes support, user training, performance monitoring, optimization, analytics, and continuous improvement. The goal is to ensure that the system is operating effectively and meeting business needs.

Here are some key tips to provide post-deployment support for Salesforce Field Service:

- *Monitor the system*: After deploying Salesforce Field Service to production, you should monitor the system to ensure that everything is working as expected. This involves monitoring system performance, data integrity, and user adoption.

- *Address issues*: If you encounter any issues or errors after deploying Salesforce Field Service to production, you should address them promptly. This involves troubleshooting the issues, identifying the root cause, and implementing a solution.

- *Provide ongoing training and support*: To ensure that your team is comfortable using Salesforce Field Service, you should provide ongoing training and support. This involves providing training materials, conducting training sessions, and providing ongoing support to help users troubleshoot issues and answer questions.

- *Implement enhancements and updates*: Salesforce Field Service is constantly evolving, and new features and updates are released regularly. To ensure that you are getting the most out of the application, you should implement enhancements and updates as they become available.

- *Collect feedback and make improvements*: To continuously improve your Salesforce Field Service deployment, you should collect feedback from users and stakeholders. This involves soliciting feedback through surveys or focus groups, analyzing the feedback, and implementing improvements based on the feedback.

- *Use analytics to track performance*: Build reports and dashboard to track key performance indicator metrics (KPIs), gain insights into your field service operations, and make data-driven decisions.

By providing post-deployment support for Salesforce Field Service, you can ensure that your team is comfortable using the application and that you are getting the most out of the application. With ongoing support and continuous improvement, you can optimize your Salesforce Field Service deployment to meet your business needs and drive business value.

Best Practices

Throughout the deployment process, it is important to follow best practices, such as aligning business requirements with technology capabilities, engaging stakeholders and users throughout the process, adopting an agile approach to implementation, leveraging Salesforce Field Service features and functionality, and measuring and reporting on success metrics.

Key Performance Metrics

Knowing and tracking KPIs regularly helps businesses to fill in the gaps in their existing field service processes thereby improving their service consistently.

The following are some of the key metrics that can help you in improving your field service process:

- *Customer satisfaction score (CSAT)*: Indicates how satisfied customers are with the services offered. The best way to calculate the CSAT is to send a survey to your customers and request that they provide feedback after every work order completion.

- *First-time fix rates (FTFRs)*: Indicates the time within which a technician is able to resolve an issue the first time, without the need for further skill, knowledge, or parts. A higher FTFR percentage indicates better performance.

To improve the FTFR percentage, ensure that your resources have 360-degree access to the following information handy from their mobile devices:

- Full job details such as customer information, site visit history, associated asset history, schedules, parts required to complete the job, estimated completion times, and estimated travel times.

- Relevant articles such as procedures, guidelines, past experiences, known issues, or video tutorials that can help resources close the task with minimum expertise.

- Offline support that can enable access to important information even when the resources are traveling or have weak network connections.

Having measures in place to manage and reduce call volume and customer wait times is critical to guaranteeing customer satisfaction (CSAT) and agent retention.

To reduce call volume consider implementing, here are some things to implement:

- A self-service customer portal on your site or your customer-facing app that can guide customers with preconfigured chatbots or knowledge articles

- Automated notifications that can send updates regarding delay, cancelations, status changes to customers automatically via email, SMS, or push notifications on the customer-facing app

- Appointment Assistant, which can allow customers to track estimated arrival time when the technicians are on their way

Improve Time to Travel indicates the amount of time spent in traveling by technicians. The less time spent on traveling, the better the time and cost effectiveness.

To reduce travel time for resources, consider the following:

- Optimize the Scheduler in such a way that the traveling time is reduced for the technician.

- Embed GPS technology into the Field Service mobile app to direct technicians to the shortest route to the site.

Reports and Dashboards Analytics

To track KPIs, you can start by installing a free package of Field Service dashboards and reports from Salesforce Labs. You can change and alter these dashboards as necessary to create performance and management dashboards that are uniquely tailored to your needs.

The app provides three dashboards for the following people:

- Service managers

- Inventory managers

- System admins

To install the dashboard package, follow these steps:

1. Navigate to appexchange.salesforce.com. Search for *Field Service Dashboards by Salesforce Labs* and click Get It Now.

2. Log in to the Salesforce org and follow the instructions for installing it.

3. Once the installation is completed, dashboards can be accessed from the Dashboards tab in the Field Service app.

Figure 8-4 shows a snapshot of the Service Manager dashboard.

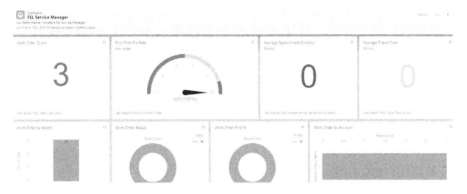

Figure 8-4. *Service Manager Dashboard*

If you want to create your own reports from scratch, use the existing report types or create a custom report type.

To create a custom report type, follow these steps:

1. From the setup, in the Quick Find box, enter **Report Types** and select Report Types.

2. Click New Custom Report Type.

3. In the Primary Object drop-down list, select any Field Service object you want to report on.

4. Enter the required fields, click Next and Save.

5. Add any related object and click Save.

6. Click Edit Layout to add or remove fields.

If you are looking for more visualizing appealing and deeper analytics, Salesforce also offers the Field Service Analytics app. Field Service Analytics offers just-in-time analytics for field service managers and dispatchers with dashboards based on your data. Field Service Analytics is part of Salesforce's CRM Analytics product. You can create a Field Service Analytics template from the CRM Analytics app.

Future Trends for Salesforce Field Service

Salesforce Field Service is likely to see an increased use of artificial intelligence and predictive analytics to optimize scheduling, improve resource allocation, and identify potential issues before they occur. This will help businesses to provide more efficient and effective service while reducing costs.

With the growing usage of mobile devices, there is likely to be a greater emphasis on the mobile capabilities in Salesforce Field Service. This may include enhanced mobile apps and interfaces, as well as the integration of new technologies such as augmented reality.

Salesforce Field Service may place more emphasis on customer experience as customers' expectations continue to change. This could involve the use of real-time notifications, personalized recommendations, and more effective scheduling.

There is likely to be greater integration between Internet of Things (IoT) data and Salesforce Field Service. This will enable businesses to proactively monitor and manage equipment, detect and diagnose issues, and optimize maintenance schedules.

As businesses seek to improve efficiency and reduce costs, there is likely to be greater collaboration between Field Service and other departments such as sales, marketing, and customer service. This will enable businesses to better align their operations and provide a more seamless experience for customers.

Summary

In summary, Salesforce Field Service deployment involves several key steps.

- Pre-deployment planning involves identifying your business needs, documenting your artifacts, planning your budget, and communicating a rollout strategy to stakeholders.

- Before deploying Salesforce Field Service to production, you should test the application in a sandbox environment to ensure that everything is working as expected. Use the Field Service Health Check tool to test your configuration by running automated tests.

- Once you have tested Salesforce Field Service thoroughly in the sandbox environment, you can deploy the application to your production environment.

- After deploying Salesforce Field Service to production, you should provide ongoing support to ensure that everything is working as expected. Provide training to your team, implement enhancements and updates, and collect feedback to continuously improve your deployment.

- Salesforce Field Service provides powerful reporting and analytics capabilities that allow you to track different KPIs, gain insights into your field service operations, and make data-driven decisions.

By following these steps and leveraging the capabilities of Salesforce Field Service, you can optimize your field service operations, improve customer satisfaction, and drive business value.

Index

A

ABC Automobiles, 34, 35, 52, 59, 153

App extensions, 187, 215–218, 241

App Launcher, 39, 48, 60, 84

Appointment Assistant, 187, 256

Autocreated service, 37

Auto-Create Service
Appointment, 53, 63

"Auto-generate work orders", 119, 130, 131

Automated notifications, 255

Automatic status changes, 206, 207

Automobile companies, 11

B

Book Appointment action, 92, 93

C

Connected app, 188, 189, 240

Customer satisfaction score
(CSAT), 254, 255

D, E

Dashboards, 256–258

Data integration rules, 46, 47, 63

Deployment process
implementation and
testing, 246–249
post-deployment
support, 252–254
pre-deployment (*see* Pre-
deployment planning)
pre-deployment planning, 244

Dispatcher console
accessing, 138
bulk actions on service
appointments, 144
candidates action, 140
dispatch action, 143
dispatcher console view, 138
as dispatcher's primary
workspace, 138
Gantt chart, 144
calendar and Gantt
Resolution drop-down
list, 145
filter service resources, 146
Gantt Locker, 146
key performance indicator
bar, 145
notifications and
optimizations requests, 147
resource utilization, 145

G, H

I, J, K

U, V

User acceptance testing (UAT), 245, 246, 248

W, X, Y, Z

Work orders, 59, 60
    articles, 61
    child, 61

line item, 26, 61
resource, 62
service appointments, 61
skills, 61
Work rules, 70
    and service
        objectives, 79
    standard, 70
    types, 70

GPSR Compliance

The European Union's (EU) General Product Safety Regulation (GPSR) is a set of rules that requires consumer products to be safe and our obligations to ensure this.

If you have any concerns about our products, you can contact us on

ProductSafety@springernature.com

In case Publisher is established outside the EU, the EU authorized representative is:

Springer Nature Customer Service Center GmbH
Europaplatz 3
69115 Heidelberg, Germany